New graphic design in Revolutionary Russia

KT-216-197

Szymon Bojko

COLLEGE LIBRARY
COLLEGE OF TECHNOLOGY
CARNARVON ROAD
SOUTHEND-ON-SEA, ESSEX

New graphic design in Revolutionary Russia

Praeger Publishers
New York · Washington

21769 X

In memory of Galina Chichagova

769.947

BOOKS THAT MATTER

Published in the United States of America in 1972
by Praeger Publishers Inc., 111 Fourth Avenue, New York, N.Y. 10003

All rights reserved
No part of this publication may be reproduced, stored in a retrieval system or
transmitted in any form or by any means, electronic, mechanical, photocopying,
recording or otherwise, without the prior permission of the Copyright owner.

Library of Congress Catalog Card Number: 72–78338

Translated from the Polish by Robert Strybel and Lech Zembrzuski
© 1972 in London, England by Lund Humphries Publishers Ltd

Printed in Great Britain

Contents

Juryi Roshkov:
Photomontage for Mayakovsky's poem:
'A temporary monument created by
Mayakovsky to the workers of Kursk who
first extracted the ore' c.1925.

Preface

Writing from the Weimar Bauhaus to Rodchenko in 1923 Moholy-Nagy
said of Constructivism 'this word has made a whirlwind career, but few
people understand its sense'. Half a century later, and despite the
enormous influence it has had on twentieth-century typography and graphic
design throughout the industrialised world, the Constructivist
contribution is inadequately recognised even by many of those designers
who have been most profoundly influenced by its achievements.
The pioneering work of some of the most gifted and imaginative Russian
designers of the revolutionary period has remained obscured. Because of
their ephemeral nature, few of the printed products of this remarkable and
vigorous band of innovators have found their way into Western archives,
while, in Russia, a creative movement that should provide a genuine source
of national pride was for many years officially ignored. Inevitably this
situation has distorted the historical record; much work of significance
has been neglected, while other works, because of their easier availability,
have been over-exposed. Any Western writer on the Russian graphic
contribution of this important period is keenly aware of the obstacles which
have frustrated attempts to arrive at a balanced assessment. It was, I
believe the particular and lasting achievement of Camilla Gray, who died
tragically in Russia at the age of 35 last year, that she succeeded in
overcoming so many of those obstacles and, through her book *The
Great Experiment*, in opening a window for Western readers and students
to one of the most vital and colourful movements in twentieth-century art
and design. This present work, too, owes much to her enthusiasm and
initiative.

Szymon Bojko, a distinguished Polish writer on the arts, who has had
regular access to archives in Moscow, now leads us into one sector of that

fertile landscape and, with the easy authority of one who is thoroughly familiar with his subject, points out its significant features. He has brought together a rich collection of illustrations to support his careful and detailed evaluation. This stimulating and penetrating work will, I believe, at last help to establish a balanced view of the immense contribution to the creation of the culture of a new society made by Russian graphic designers during one of the most socially exciting periods of European history.

Herbert Spencer

Introduction

There has hitherto been no systematic account of the history of applied graphic art in Russia during the period of the Revolution and immediately thereafter.

The new currents in painting and the intellectual movements surrounding the new revolutionary art have been far better treated. Non-permanent art-forms, with the possible exception of the poster, have been sadly neglected by historians and critics alike. Practical difficulties, multiplied by the fact that few such art-works have survived, have been largely responsible for this state of affairs. Owing to unsystematic archives, incomplete collections, the lack of original printer's copies and the sizeable number of unattributable works, a prospective researcher is confronted by a mountain of unknowns. In order to reconstruct a logical whole and maintain scholarly objectivity, a researcher in this field must carefully avoid the pitfall of over-simplified *a priori* assessments with which literature of the 1920's and 1930's on Soviet art abounded.

The present sketch has no exceedingly ambitious goals. The principal aim is to introduce some semblance of order into existing research, and to reflect upon some of the already verified but generally less accessible artistic phenomena. Little attempt is made critically to evaluate the current state of research, even though this might seem the logical point to begin.

Of the works published prior to World War II, the commentary of a new-art spokesman, N. Punin, in an album of posters by V. Lebedev, should first of all be mentioned. The monograph by V. Polonsky on revolutionary posters, published in 1925, was a treatise dealing with Cubo-Futurism and a critique of the search for new artistic forms. The erudite essays of Prof. A. Sidorov on book illustration and those of E. Gollerbach tend to underestimate the influence of the *avant-garde* on the revival of applied art.

Post-war literature pertinent to this subject increased substantially. The penetrating study by N. Khardzhiyev on El Lissitzky, and numerous works appearing in the periodical *Decorative Art in the USSR* (Dekorativnoye Iskusstvo SSR) on A. Rodchenko, L. Popova, V. Tatlin, the Stenberg Brothers and G. Klutsis have shed a great deal of light on the creative achievements of these artists in the field of the graphic arts.

Of those works published outside the Soviet Union it is worth mentioning the monograph on Lissitzky prepared by his wife, Sophie Lissitzky-Küppers, and published originally in the German Democratic Republic. Also worth noting is Camilla Gray's work entitled *The Great Experiment: Russian Art 1863–1922* as well as two of that author's articles on Lissitzky and Rodchenko published in *Typographica*. The subject is also dealt with by Herbert Spencer in *Pioneers of Modern Typography*, and in a special issue of the Czechoslovak periodical *Vytvarné Umeni* (8/9 1967). Polish works in this field have included B. Lewandowska's *U źródeł grafiki funkcjonalnej w Polsce* (The sources of applied graphic art in Poland) as well as a number of articles prepared by me and published in the periodicals *Projekt* and *Fotografia*.

In recent years a number of substantial exhibitions which have contributed to the reconstruction of art-objects and documents not generally accessible have given additional impetus to this research. A new iconography has thus come to the fore, making it possible to venture beyond the usual stock of familiar quotations and names. This has also cleared the field of historical introspection. In this connexion mention might be made first and foremost of the exhibition 'Mass Agitation Art of the Early Years of the Revolution', first shown in Moscow's Tretiakov Gallery in 1967, and subsequently in Prague. The acclaim it received both from the general public and specialists showed that it had filled a gap in a field which continues to be the subject of heated debate. In the same year Warsaw was the scene of a retrospective exhibition entitled 'International Revolutionary Posters'. Through the use of exhibits borrowed from various European museums and collections a confrontation of socially engaged art was staged on a scale without precedent. The same exhibition was shown at Stockholm's Moderna Museet in 1968, where it was acclaimed by critics as an artistic event *par excellence*. Two exhibitions held in the Russian Museum at Leningrad helped to reassess the revolutionary graphic tradition. They were entitled 'Russian Graphics in the Late 19th and Early 20th Centuries', the fruit of the studies on the beginnings of modern art in Russia conducted by the outstanding art historian E. Kovtun, and the 'Petrograd Windows of Rosta' (1968) which brought to light the little-known street posters of Petrograd from the civil war and intervention period. By contrast, such exhibitions as 'Werbegrafik 1920–1930' at Frankfurt am Main, 'Awangarda 1910–1930 Osteuropa' organized by Berlin's Kunstverein in 1967, and a display known as 'Die Fotomontage' which toured a number of cities in the German Federal Republic in 1969, were of lesser significance as regards further broadening of our knowledge in this area.

Important artistic events of the last few years have included, among others, an exhibition of G. Klutsis's works organized by the Art Museum in Riga (1970), and the 'Art in Revolution' exhibition – shown at the Hayward Gallery in London early in 1971 and subsequently toured, in a much reduced and primarily documentary form, in North America and Europe – which was an ambitious attempt at presenting a synthetic view of the art of the revolutionary period. Little-known museum items were exhibited within the 'Russian Art of the Revolution' display organized by the Brooklyn Museum of Art (1971).

Having embarked in the introduction on a presentation of the history of graphic art in the revolutionary period, we should, first of all, determine what we mean by 'new graphic art'. It is a rather all-embracing term, and we have therefore settled on two conventional guidelines.

The first is concerned with the scope and limits of graphic art and more or less encompasses what in today's terminology would be classified as mass media: books and illustrations, illustrated periodicals, posters, advertisements, etc. Apart from these applications, graphic art – conceived as a classic discipline – should be defined as a form of artistic expression related to painting. And yet, the matter is not all that straightforward and simple. When printing was basically an inaccessible luxury, a woodcut or linocut stood in for the printing industry which was still virtually non-existent. When the woodcut left the domain of serious, collector's editions of books, it sought refuge in inexpensive children's books and adorned the covers of periodicals and scientific publications. But the autonomy of form, as determined by material, tool and technique, was responsible for the fact that graphic art remained outside the mainstream of the transformations taking place in the field of art. Graphic artists continued the traditions of the preceding epochs, although some of the more outstanding practitioners in the field did begin to respond to what had taken place in contemporary art. And so, for example, traces of the Cubist approach to spatial organization did appear in the early works of Favorsky. The theory of composition taught by him in the basic course at the Vkhutemas[1] contained numerous concepts which coincided with and were analogous to Constructivist views. While exerting an influence on the entire younger generation of graphic artists by virtue of his individualism, Favorsky was nevertheless criticized by the school's academic youth for the conservatism of his thinking. The faculty of graphic art headed by

Favorsky was the scene of a debate on artistic principles. The following is an excerpt from a student newspaper of 1922: 'We left-wing Constructivists did not enter the graphics faculty in order to dwell there peacefully. Do not speak such nonsense, comrades! We state that we came there so that, having encircled the faculty with a metal ring, we might weed out eclecticism and routine aesthetics. Comrade graphic artists, you have forgotten what a machine really is!'[2]

The second guideline is of an ideational nature. The new graphic art was a part of the transformations which had been taking place in Russian art of the early twentieth century. Cubo-Futurism had grown up on the ruins of Modernism[3] and the already fossilized painting of the Pyeredvizhniki.[4] It gave rise to radical tendencies which called into question the entire existing aesthetic legacy. These tendencies were Constructivism and Suprematism which grew out of the same seed as Neo-Plasticism and geometric abstraction. The two artistic groups representing these tendencies had in common the aim of revolutionizing art. They were divided, however, on the question of the function of art in society. Whereas the Constructivists elevated the concept of utilitarianism to the highest artistic virtue, Suprematism strove to free art of the burden of objectivity and to limit it to categories of pure feeling. The substance of the controversy can be illustrated by this brief extract from the ideological debate:

Chuzhak: 'Art, if it is proletarian art, we consider as something temporary, until it finally merges with life and takes the form of activity which harnesses emotions so as to impart to the class and humanity the value of needed things.' Malevich: 'All those who advocate the construction of useful and practical "things", and who oppose or seek to subjugate the arts should bear in mind that there exist no practical, constructed "things".'[5]

Were these differences that were voiced in verbal duels and theory confirmed in creative practice? A researcher can offer only a qualified yes. It is true, however, that utilitarian forms in ceramics and furniture developed by N. Suetin and I. Chashnik, the pupils closest to Malevich, traced their ancestry directly to Suprematism.

None the less, despite certain doctrinaire tendencies, the historical achievement of the Constructivists, 'proizvodstvienniki'[6] and advocates of industrial art was the fact that they consistently opposed the nineteenth-century distinction between fine and applied art. They put into practice the modern ideal of the universality and unity of art – the unity of aesthetic experience and of mastering reality. It is for this reason that, without belittling the contributions of many artists of the 1920's, such as Favorsky or Kravchenko, this study will concentrate on the achievements and ideas of the *avant-garde*.

At the source

The link between Futurist poetry and Cubist art, growing as in other European countries out of the artistic rebellion, constitutes the lineage of the new graphic art and typography.

Poets from 'Gileya'[7] and painters representing such groups as 'Osliniy Khvost' (Donkey's Tail)[8] and 'Soyuz Molodyozhy' (League of Youth)[9] joined in the attack on common sense. The Philistines were astonished by world-shaking proclamations, and authorities became the objects of ridicule. The destruction of everything connected with classical style, orthography, syntax and verse construction was predicted. The titles of manifestoes caused scandals, and the graphic means employed were clearly provocative. For example, the declaration-manifesto 'Pashchochina obshchestviennomu vkusu' (The Insult to Universal Taste)[10] was printed on poor quality packing paper. Verbal audacity accompanied each unceremonious reckoning with the aestheticism cultivated by artists associated with 'Mir Isskustva' (World of Art). In addition to the provocative slogan 'Throw Pushkin, Dostoevsky, Tolstoy, etc. from the steam-ship of contemporaneity' the concept of a beautiful book was undermined. The so-called manual books made a mockery of meticulously ornate illustrations and decorations and parodied exceedingly 'tasteful' type-styles as well as, indirectly, the entire aesthetics of Modernism. These books appeared meteorically outside of the normal book market. They were financed by the authors themselves as playthings, much in the spirit of Dadaism, partly for the purpose of demonstrating artistic independence.

'Anti-books' embodied the precepts of Cubo-Futurism. Futurist poets maintained that a word's pictorial designation must be as active as the word itself. Between the written word, the sound of speech and the graphic form of the letter-symbol there exists an interdependence which influences the quality of perception. The even precision of printer's type makes a text monotonous and expressionless; by contrast, the free rhythm of manually composed letters, synchronized with a given text, can convey the spirit and mood of a literary work. V. Khlebnikov went farthest as regards the formal construction of a word. In the essay *Bukva kak takovaya* (A Letter as Such)[11] Khlebnikov stated that the particular cut of the type used is capable of registering each and every change of emotional climate. The shape of the letters, moreover, can convey a definite mood to the reader regardless of the words being used. Unable to achieve the artistry of a word through machine-printing, the Futurists preferred hand-made symbols derived from ancient prints, incunabula, the Bible and medieval codexes.

In the years 1912–14 more than twenty books were printed by the lithographic method. The handicraft character of the production was apparent throughout. Drawings were placed at random on the page. The text styled with careful carelessness at times turned into an illustration. A casual and direct contact with the reader was suggested by the cheap, generally rough-textured grey or brown paper used, with pages of irregular size and shape. Occasionally authors would tint lithographs by hand, without observing the contours, a feature reminiscent of folk pictures. A wealth of concepts and colours was represented by a volume of poetry entitled *Telile* by A. Kruchyonykh and Khlebnikov designed by O. Rozanova (1914). Kruchyonykh published a number of small books in collaboration with painters, and one of them, a mere leaflet, he designed himself with the self-irony so typical of his works. The leaflet was basically a collage composed of bits of coloured paper cut into simple geometric forms bearing typewritten word-exclamations. For another book entitled *Pomade* (1913), illustrated by Larionov, Kruchyonykh provided a commentary of 'three words written in his own language, differing from the rest in that they have no meaning'. An example of a Dadaist pure nonsense attempt appears below:
No.1 Dir-bul-shchyl

   ube sh shchur

   skum

   vy so bu

   r–l ez

The creation of a climate of improvisation and honesty seems to be the essential point behind these poetic, artistic and editorial pursuits. Kruchyonykh demanded complete authenticity. 'Let a book be plain, but without deceit; everything that belongs in that book must be authentic, to the very last blot.'[12] Malevich was another of the authors of the lithographic books. Not without significance is the hitherto little-known fact that Malevich also published *Suprematism* (Vitebsk, 1920), a short treatise in which he expounded the bases of his aesthetic theory of an auto-lithographic technique which retained manual printing. The cover of a collection of verse *Troye*

(Khlebnikov, Kruchyonykh, J. Guro) may provide a clue as to his inspiration to use Old-Church-Slavonic script, although the form of prismatically cut letters would seem to indicate a certain affinity with analytical Cubism. It might be said that the evocations of 'Les demoiselles d'Avignon' blend with Russian folklore. In commenting on the beginnings of the new typography Lissitzky expressed the opinion that these inexpensive and unbound lithographic notebooks 'should be treated as folk art despite the fact of their urban origin'.[13] This guideline was most essential, for not all studies had distinguished between the two trends of unprofessional folk art which had had a significant influence on the Russian variant of Cubism. The first, the traditional lubok,[14] was the product of the peasant imagination still untainted by civilization; the other was the folklore which developed in large centres of population, laying the groundwork for mass culture. Shop signs, photographer's screens, pictures sold at town markets, paintings hanging in second-rate restaurants – all that production on the borderline between art and trash, so despised by aesthetes, generated the admiration of the Futurists. Moreover, it in no wise undermined their vision of technical progress in their backward land, for primitive art enabled them to make an enchanted pilgrimage to the genesis of culture, to the birth-place of the myth. It recaptured the primeval spectacular quality of an object of the imagination and its folk function of play and magic. Naïve and free from literary allusion, it communicated in a visual code reminiscent of the symbols used by primitive man who left traces of his spiritual existence on the walls of his cave.

Tin signs, whose subjects were so exquisitely portrayed, the lubok depicting moralities and philosophical precepts, the icon merging earthly and heavenly matters in a single abstract, artistic space – such were the elements of folk culture and religious art, deeply rooted in the Russian soil, that strangely merged with the art of the oncoming age of electricity, technology and great scientific discovery.

N. Suetin was to write many years later: 'Russian art in its most characteristic periods was always alive with that which originated in the rural community: nature, fields, forest. This is not to say that it will always remain so, but one should not overlook this fact on its road to development.'[15]

Graphic design and typography in the theory of Constructivism

The theoretical justifications of the new typography and graphic art must be pieced together from incidental statements, for they do not comprise a cohesive system which could be designated as a theory.

The Russian Constructivists, as opposed to their West European colleagues associated with the Bauhaus, de Stijl or the Polish *avant-garde*, seldom formulated theoretical views on mass-media art. An exception to the rule was Lissitzky, who assumed the role of revolutionary commentator and ideologist, similar to the one played by Mayakovsky in literature.

The epoch delighted in manifestoes and programmatic declarations. Lissitzky issued the ideological credo of typography in an article entitled 'The typography of typography'.[16] In some respects it was reminiscent of the 'Realistic Manifesto' of Pevsner and Gabo. It contained the following points:

1. Printed words are seen and not heard.
2. Thoughts are communicated by the appropriate words and formed by letters of the alphabet.
3. Thoughts should be expressed with maximum economy, optically not phonetically.
4. The composition of text on a page is governed by the laws of typographical mechanics – it should reflect the flow and rhythm of the contents.
5. Illustrative material should be used to organize a page in accordance with the new visual theory.
6. A sequence of pages is a cinematographic book.
7. A new book requires new means of writing – the ink-well and quill are a thing of the past.
8. A printed book has conquered time and space. Printed pages and the infinity of books must be conquered. Electro-library.

It is certainly not difficult to find here a continuation of the concept of the visual values of writings developed by the creators of lithographic books, although Lissitzky had precluded any type of manual activity. He was of the opinion that a revolution in the traditional book could be achieved by industrial printing, but he did borrow from the Futurists their ideas on optimum visual stimuli. As a newly appointed lecturer on typography at the School of Fine Arts at Vitebsk (1919–20), he experimented with a 'visual book' constructed by mechanical means. Since the sense of sight is the one most involved in the reading process ('a book is conveyed to the brain by means of the eye and not the ear'), he came to the conclusion that the art of printing is a factor which accumulates and transmits energy, and its basic substance is type. The shape, size, proportion and composition of type against a background are not independent of the substance being conveyed, but rather they regulate a word's emotional and intellectual reception. Later he was to write on this subject on two different occasions. Since the article 'Unser Buch' has been included in the monograph on the artist,[17] we might recall a lesser-known text from the guide-book *All-Union Polygraphic Exhibition* (Moscow, 1927). The excerpt cited below is characteristic of the experiences of that period. 'Until the revolution our artists neglected the composition of print. It was only after the revolution that artists, striving as they did in every discipline to find the appropriate artistic substance of that discipline, began creating a new type of book out of typographic material. These endeavours moved in two directions. The first aimed at achieving a book's "architecture", i.e. programming the whole as well as individual pages. Designing in line with this concept was based on the proportions and relationship of a page's individual elements, the relationship of the typographical composition to the paper area, the contrast and size of type, and most importantly the exclusive use of typographical material and specific printing processes, e.g. colour overlap. In the second tendency, which might be called artistic montage, most essential was the use of print composition as a building material for assembling a cover, individual pages, and posters. Both tendencies are directly linked to production . . . Contemporary polygraphy is entering a phase which will produce changes in composition technique similar to those which took place in manuscripts after Gutenberg's invention. The levers of that revolution were light and physical chemistry, or that which leads in consequence to photo-mechanics. Just as radio put an end to telegraph poles, cables and telegraph stations, so too will photo-mechanics free us from metal type, plates, etc.'

In his theoretical deliberations Lissitzky was a proponent of the doctrine of functionalism. He applied it to mass-produced utility articles, whether furniture or newspapers. In both instances he showed a preference for that which was permanent, purposeful, economic and objective – for the antithesis of chance or a subjective play of imagination beyond the control of intellect. In predicting the course printing development would take, he underlined the interdependence between technological progress and elementary forms. He considered standardization and unification not as an evil, but as an inevitable stage of civilization – an introduction to the aesthetics of the industrial era.

We have learnt of Mayakovsky's views on graphic art from his dispute with V. Polonsky, representing the conservative wing of art criticism. A successive wave of attacks on *Lef* in 1927 prompted the poet to come to the defence of both the graphic form of writing and its author, Rodchenko. Mayakovsky recalled that 'Rodchenko, keeping abreast of technology, in the pages of *Lef*[18] for the first time put aside his pen and pencil to take up photomontage. That was in 1923, and at present the use of photomontage and illustrations in the manner of Rodchenko is widely recommended in the press. In the past three years he has given graphic art a completely new orientation. Rodchenko has created a new style in book covers.'[19] This somewhat affected reply was a bit imprecise. It would be impossible to ascribe the modernization of printing exclusively to Rodchenko, and associating the style created by him with photomontage was a blatant oversimplification. The turning-point initiated by Lissitzky, Rodchenko, Gan and others expressed itself in the severance of ties with historical styles and in the use of design methods in typography.

Rodchenko, as many-sided a talent as Lissitzky, exhibited the greatest independence, spirit of discovery and inventiveness in the field of typography and photography. We do not know, however, of any documents produced by him on the theoretical bases of graphic design. Perhaps this resulted from his lack of a predilection for abstract thinking. He was reported as having confessed: 'I have great difficulties with writing, for I think in pictures.' He veered instead in the direction of methodology in which he felt himself to be on more solid ground. He was author of numerous programmes at Vkhutemas, conducted a Constructivism seminar at the theatrical school under Meyerhold, and participated in the work of the Institute of Artistic Culture.[20]

His methodological materials can serve as an indirect source of information on Rodchenko's views, on the cognitive and philosophical aspects of design, and on the personality traits of the artist-constructor.

In the Vkhutemas 'Construction Course' programme (*c.*1922–3) mention was made of the intellectual and professional qualifications of an industrial designer: a critical attitude towards the surrounding world of things, a sense of inventiveness, perceptivity, an explorer's initiative, a willingness constantly to improve and simplify objects, and a feeling for variety. 'An inventive proposal and not merely a project is what is expected of a designer.' Mentioned among the didactic goals in the introduction to a programme 'Basic Division' are, among other things, the development of the ability simultaneously to accept coloured, linear and kinetic impressions, approaching optical impressions not as externally occurring movement, but as taking place within a subject's internal world (tension, mood changes).[21] Rodchenko, the Constructivist, considers physical, internal and psychical reality as a dynamic system subject to infinite transformations. He places the artist in the role of an observer – one who discloses the new facets and aspects of that reality. In the debate that developed with the proponents of static photography Rodchenko spoke out in favour of training the eye simultaneously to perceive visual impressions from all sides, since such an attitude corresponded to the consciousness of contemporary man. 'In order to teach man to gaze unconventionally, it is necessary to photograph ordinary, familiar objects from totally unexpected vantage points and in unexpected combinations; by contrast, new objects should be photographed from various perspectives, giving a full impression of their appearance . . . While taught to look in a routine and traditional manner, we must discover the visible world anew. We must revolutionize our visual thinking. We must remove the cataract from our eyes . . .'[22]

The motifs of relative perception, changeable form, and changing, revolutionary reality were recurring themes in the basic concepts propagated by the *avant-garde*.
CONSTRUCTIVISM IS THE CONTEMPORARY WORLD OUTLOOK.
THERE EXISTS NO ETERNAL ART.
ALL IS SUBJECT TO CHANGE.
CONSTRUCTIVE LIFE IS THE ART OF THE FUTURE.

These are some of the statements incorporated in posters by Vkhutemas students, as recorded by Rodchenko in his recollections of Mayakovsky. 'We were rebelling against accepted canons, techniques, tastes and values . . . We had a vision of a new world, industry, technology and science. We were inventors and transformers of the world . . . We created new concepts of beauty and broadened the concept of art itself . . . We were opposed because of our slogans of "Death to art, long live production!" We were taken to task for not recognizing "pure art", for being printers, photographers, designers of fabrics and shop displays – because we made graphic layouts for newspapers.[23]

The defiant slogan-challenge, which was to cause so many later misunderstandings, appeared on the first page of Alexei Gan's brochure *Constructivism*, published in the provincial town of Tver (1922): 'We are declaring unmitigated war on Art!'

The two lines were set in 20-point lower-case and heavily underscored. Below, the authors are named: the First Working Group of Constructivists, Moscow, 1920.

On the basis of this, his sole publication, Gan found a place in the history of Constructivism, becoming the group's ideologist in the eyes of researchers. But was he really, or did such a notion take root merely owing to circumstances? It is difficult to provide a documented reply to that question, as Gan left behind only sparse information for posterity. It has proved impossible to reconstruct his life history, or to ascertain the year of his birth, or the date and circumstances of his death. Nothing is known about his academic studies, and the possibility of him being self-educated has not been discounted. He wrote articles on theatre, including Meyerhold's presentations, he was involved in typography, was familiar with printing, photography, cinema – he designed kiosks and display pavilions. He was editor and publisher of a weekly, *Kinofot*, and did the *mise en page* for the journal *Sovremiennaya Arkhitektura*. From scattered information it would appear that Gan exerted an influence on artistic life. A doctrinaire fanatic, a Robespierre of Constructivism, he was under constant critical fire from the opponents of the new art. He was cited as evidence of the extreme ideological nihilism of the entire *avant-garde*.

Gan pointed out in the introduction that the brochure had been published for the purpose of agitation and war with proponents of traditional art. For an historian this fact can undoubtedly serve as a hint that the theses contained therein should be treated with a certain caution. Such caution was recommended by Camilla Gray, who referred her readers desirous of becoming acquainted with the ideology of Constructivism to the writings of Brik, Kushner, Meyerhold and *Lef*.[24]

We are primarily concerned with Gan's publication as a characteristic document of the epoch and of a particular type of print. We have here an example of a poster approach to complex problems of cultural theory, and of the theory and sociology of art. Analysis of the subject, the presentation of evidence, and the conclusions and judgements are provided in the form of slogans, both from the linguistic as well as the visual point of view. The most important closing portion of the publication contains an exposition of Constructivism – a triad:

Tectonics	a concept borrowed from geological terminology, used here to designate the organic unity of ideology and form.
Fracture treatment	or the state and behaviour of material and the manner in which it is shaped.
Construction	the creative process.

The author imparted an extremely evocative printed form to his argument and was accused of oversimplification and vulgar sociologism. The differentiation of the size, thickness and cut of the type, the staggering of serif and sans serif type, and spacing – all of these are familiar and rather elementary printing techniques, but they were subordinated to the text in conformity with the principles of the triad.

From the standpoint of style, even more characteristic is another manifesto with the high-sounding title 'Constructivists of the World'. It was signed by a three-man team also calling itself the First Working Group of Constructivists (a competitor of Gan), i.e. by K. Medunetzky and the brothers V. and G. Stenberg, of whom the two latter were later to become outstanding poster artists. It was published on the occasion of an exhibition in Moscow (January 1920). This document also makes mention of 'declaring war on art'.

On the subject of photomontage we have only one major statement to go on, that of Gustav Klutsis. It dates from 1913, a period when Constructivism was beginning to descend from the historical stage. Klutsis presented the genealogy of this genre and its development in the Soviet Union, described the artistic language of photomontage, and emphasized its connexion both with politics and with industrial and technological progress. 'Photomontage, as the newest method of plastic art, is closely linked to the development of industrial culture and of forms of mass cultural media.' . . . 'There arises a need for art whose force would be a technique armed with apparatus and chemistry, MEETING THE STANDARDS OF SOCIALIST INDUSTRY. Photomontage has turned out to be such an art.'[25]

Both in the theoretical sphere and in their creative production the Russian Constructivists took up problems which were exercising European graphic art at that time. They belonged to the same branch of the *avant-garde* which, beginning with the Cubist revolution, thoroughly upset accepted notions about objects and broke down the traditional limitations of material and technique, proposing instead a new shape for graphic art and new poetics. 'Art is dead – long live the new machine art of Tatlin' proclaimed a poster at the 1920 exhibition in Berlin. The collage 'Tatlin at home' hanging next to it had about it the gesture of an alliance between German Dadaism and Russian Constructivism.

Functional typography was influenced on the one hand by Dadaism, on the other by Constructivist orientations – Purism, Neo-Plasticism, the Bauhaus, Czech and Polish Constructivist thinking. The affinity of Polish and Russian centres becomes most evident when analysing the programmatic utterances, texts and graphic lay-out of the periodical *Blok*, the organ of the Polish *avant-garde* published in the years 1924–6.

A lively relationship existed between such centres of the new art as Berlin, Dessau, Amsterdam, Paris, Milan, Rome, Prague, Warsaw, Moscow, and Leningrad, and this despite the isolation in which the proletarian state found itself in the early years following the Revolution.

There is no need to reiterate the facts documenting various types of contacts, since they have already been exhaustively treated in literature. We might note some others, however—those less frequently referred to. Our interest centres primarily round the knowledge of contemporary literature and works of art in post-revolutionary Russia.

Many and varied were the roads travelled by world publications, books and periodicals. The following is what Rodchenko had to say on the subject in his recollections of Mayakovsky already referred to: 'Mayakovsky often travelled abroad, on the average four times a year. After each journey he would bring back suitcases filled with books, periodicals, advertising materials, posters, photographs, postcards and reproductions of art works. After making use of them in the press, he would distribute all the materials to his friends according to their particular interests. This distribution took place in the room of Osya [i.e. Osya Brik – author] which took on the appearance of a store. Zhemchuzhny took materials relating to theatre and cinema, Lavinsky – those dealing with architecture and sculpture, and I took art and photography. He gave me many monographs on Gross, Larionov, Goncharova, Delaunay, Rousseau's "Negroes", Picabia, A. Lothe, V. Grigoriev, Picasso. Once he brought from Paris photographic paper, a gift to me from the famous Man Ray. That was an innovation at that time – paper on a transparent base. Man Ray made photograms. On another occasion he gave me two Picasso lithographs which he had received from the artist personally. In this way, thanks to Mayakovsky, we had a steady flow of information on the culture and art of the West. And he brought with him not only the West's art, but its life, atmosphere and daily affairs with all its rays and shadows.'

Publications from the 'Bauhausbücher' series were well known and studied, particularly Moholy-Nagy's work *Malerei, Photographie, Film*. The shelves of the Vkhutemas library were graced by books that were gifts from the Bauhaus (according to Rector Novitzky), or were imported for foreign currency. Only a detail, and yet how essential it is for an understanding of the intellectual climate. Even in periods of want following the civil war, funds were allotted for the import of specialized literature and periodicals for the university.

While on the subject of the Bauhaus, it might be useful to add some facts on that school's contacts with artists from the Vkhutemas circle. Moholy-Nagy's letter written at Weimar to Rodchenko (1923) has survived.[26] It contains mention that a series of books devoted to current art problems had been started. They were to be prefaced by a discussion on Constructivism. 'This word has made a whirlwind career, but few people understand its sense', wrote Moholy-Nagy, suggesting to Rodchenko that he present the view of Russian artists on this subject. Lissitzky, during his protracted foreign sojourns, maintained contacts with numerous artistic communities in the West as a representative of Moscow's Inkhuk. Brik also made a special journey to Germany for the purpose of establishing contacts (1923). When he presented his report at Inkhuk, he announced various possibilities of co-operation, not excluding publication. It should be mentioned that *The Story of Two Squares* was printed by Scythia Verlag in Berlin and *For reading out loud* was published by the Berlin firm of Lutze & Vogt. Both publications will be discussed at length below. The establishment in 1922 of a periodical *Veshch – Objet – Gegenstand*, published in Berlin under the editorship of Lissitzky and Ilya Ehrenburg, had an almost symbolic aura about it. The introductory article in the first issue began with the words 'The blockade of Russia is ending . . .'. Despite its short lifespan (only three issues appeared), the periodical was a germ, drawing together the revolutionary art of Russia and that of progressive segments of the creative intelligentsia in the West.

Books, prints

In opposition to the ornate and baroque printing characteristic of the Modernist school, functional typography offered asceticism. The groundwork for this change had been laid by the lithographic books of the Futurists.

In conformity with the rules of Constructivism, condensed prints (i.e. books, periodicals, brochures, etc.) were to feature an economy of material, as well as of the technical and expressive resources used: a maximum of functionalism with a minimum outlay of energy. The use of drawn, painted or engraved illustrations and covers was to decline. All artistic elements were to be the product of mechanical technology or photo-mechanical processing. Straight lines and elementary forms were thought best to correspond to mechanical printing. In line with this thinking a repertoire of geometric and abstract forms was created. The use of such typographic figures as circles, squares, triangles and heavy lines became widespread. They served to order and divide the page area, and to some extent fulfilled the function of word-commentary pictograms. Strictly speaking, only one style of type was propagated (especially for titles): massive block letters of the type used in stamps, with sharply cut corners and sans serif. At a certain point in time such a fount of type was considered to be a sign of modernity and formalism . . . The following is a small but illustrative example. *Arkhitektura*, the organ of the Moscow Association of Architects, with a conservative bent, appeared in early 1923 (No.1–2) with a changed and Constructivist cover. Igor Grabar reacted to this by reprimanding the author: 'A. A. Vesnin – the extreme left wing of the Russian artistic community. A pleasant, charming, extremely capable and conscientious person. Like an infant he has become the victim of his own, blind, typically Russian "belief in an idea".'[27]

The earliest publications in the functional vein were produced at Vitebsk, the bastion of Suprematism, which almost sounds like a paradox. Lissitzky had been unable to resist the overpowering Suprematist vision of the square. But when in 1920 he began designing his *Story of Two Squares*, he added to that vision his own architectural-painting experiment brought over from *Proun*. The building substance of this odd thesis-book was an area of paper conceived in a painter's manner, with flat and three-dimensional geometric figures organized in the rhythm of film frames. The type-face, in extremely economical dosage, became a major artistic component. *For reading out loud* (*Dlya Golossa*) was another work with experimental traits. Owing to its function (the book was a selection of Mayakovsky's verse meant for recitation) Lissitzky gave it the form of an index. It was the antithesis of an illustrated book. On a total of sixty-four pages the author demonstrated all the possible combinations of the modern *mise en page* typographic technique. On the same basis of an index Lissitzky produced the Polygraphic Exhibition guidebook in co-operation with Solomon Telingater. In it he introduced a colour code for designating individual sections – in other words, a system of visual identification, as it would be called today. Incidentally, the exhibition's documentation (which has survived but has yet to receive scholarly treatment) was an example of modern, complex thinking. This included the printed rules and bulletins as well as the architectural design and artistic decoration. On a smaller scale, with a view not only to clarity and total impact but also to the 'cinematography' of print, he designed the graphic layout of the periodical *Veshch*, *Asnova* (1926) – the bulletin of the New Architecture Association – and the book *Die Kunstismen* (1925). These works allow Lissitzky to be ranked among the most outstanding typographers of the twentieth century.

The programme of Constructivism aimed at the overthrow of the division between utility, artistic pursuits and free expression – between the unique and duplicated work. The realization of this aesthetic ideal in the field of typography was the great achievement of Rodchenko which was cordially acclaimed by Mayakovsky. It was Rodchenko who elevated mass printing – book covers and ordinary brochures, the wrappers of poor quality sweets, newspaper advertisements, labels and film leaders – to the rank of genuine graphic art. The many book covers designed by Rodchenko coupled popular and legible graphics with inventive eye-attacking form. One of the first books to sport such a cover was the little tome *Mayakovsky Smiles . . .* (1923). Its novelty lies in the fact that it encouraged one to read the verse of the popular poet set out in an aggressive and visually striking manner. It aptly conveyed a youthful mood of world-shaking poetry sparkling with humour and irony. On his covers Rodchenko generally featured the photographs of persons or objects and/or cuttings from periodicals, old prints or advertising brochures. Photography complemented the lettering (*Kinofot*, No.1, 1922); it was a document, sign and symbol (*Pro Eto*, 1923; *Dayosh*, No.9, 1929) – an autonomous artistic value (*Syfilis*, 1926; *Novi Lef*, No.11/12, 1927), or a background, an element of simulated space (*Sergieyu Yesieninu*, 1923, *Narodnye massy v russkoy revolucyi*, 1923). The typo-collage and photo-collage techniques paved the way to pure experiments in the field of utilitarian tasks. In designing the cover of an almanac of Constructivist poetry *Miena Vsiekh* (1924), Rodchenko turned out as many as ten different variants, each of which embodies the unique values of a study on the borderline of photography and graphics. The covers of a series of detective stories entitled *Mess Mend* (1924) showed that the Constructivists did not despise the reader of entertainment literature. Individual books in the series bearing such sensational titles as *Corpse in the Cupboard* gave the new and inexperienced reader the satisfaction of becoming acquainted with modern graphics deliberately designed to appeal in the market-place. After all, this was not a case of aesthetic satisfaction, but rather of mutual fun and entertainment. How else could the advertisements in three cheap, one-kopeck booklets be called, designed as they were meticulously but obviously with tongue in cheek?

Rodchenko was a member of the *Lef* group and was its permanent art director. He supplied it with covers, photo-montages and photographs. He developed the external appearance of this leading periodical of the *avant-garde*. *Lef* became a pattern and a norm – one which generated both approval and opposition. It seems that the artistic works it contained should also be approached from this model point of view. Let us take, for example, the title page of *Lef* (No.1, 1923). Its lettering composition is enclosed in an extended rectangle, constructed like a piece of architecture with accented vertical axes, with heavy, handmade block letters coupled with type-fount letters. The composition is purist, conveying the impression of a machine-made mass-produced article which without exaggeration can be considered a prototype of Constructivist graphic art.

In a concise sketch it is virtually impossible to discuss fully the exceptionally prolific typographic creations of Rodchenko, his long years of co-operation with the illustrated monthly *SSSR na Stroykie* (1933–41), or his numerous albums including *Piervaya Konna* (1937).

Neither Rodchenko nor Lissitzky created an actual school of graphic art, as Favorsky had done. Nevertheless, they managed to gain young followers from amongst Vkhutemas graduates sympathetic to the new-art movement who accepted the thinking and artistic methods of their teachers. Of them, the closest to the doctrine of Constructivism were the sisters G. and O. Chichagova, L. Sanina, A. Akhtyrko, E. Semionova, G. Miller, and V. Shestakov. The Chichagova sisters were particularly active in the field of designing children's books in collaboration with the writer N. Smirnov. In the years 1923–9 about twenty such books were published, all having a uniform binding and devoted to a variety of didactic subjects as, for example, *Where*

Do Utensils Come From? (1923–4), *To the Children About Newspapers* (1924), *How People Travel* (1925), and *What's Made of What?* (1927). These were works full of striking simplicity and honesty of purpose which could both teach and amuse. They taught their young readers to look at the world rationally and to extract the essential from the things and phenomena observed. Schematic drawings similar to ideograms served as illustrations; they approximated to a child's imagination, but were never infantile. The pages were composed from type which was, of course, simple, geometric and angular, and heavier or lighter depending on the subject-matter. This terseness, the conscious form and glaring colours made the books of the Chichagova sisters akin to posters.

S. Telingater was a member of the second generation of graphic artists whose attitudes had been moulded by post-revolutionary conditions. He collaborated with Lissitzky and learnt practical knowledge from the experiences of the pioneers. He also called himself a book constructor. He did not share, however, the masters' doctrinaire faith in functionalism. He even deviated from certain principles which they had held sacred. He was not satisfied with simply the architectonics and beauty of typographical material itself. He dreamt of a 'bioscopic' book, a 'cine-book' which could be read and viewed simultaneously – one in which the sequence of pages and pictures would be reminiscent of moving-picture frames. He attempted to implement such a concept in designing a book entitled *Komsomolya* (1928), a poem written by A. Bezymiensky in honour of the tenth anniversary of the Komsomol.[28] The book developed like a film on the basis of a screenplay, and subsequently a detailed script. The creative team was composed of director, scenographer, photographer and cameraman. The montage was achieved by Telingater himself who deserves credit for directing the project as a whole. The rich visual language of the book was composed of both documentary pictures and photographs especially posed for the occasion and woven into the text, coloured accents scattered about the columns, complicated schemes of type-founts of various cut and size – and, finally, various decorative elements from the printer's moulds. To a certain extent *Komsomolya* summed up the heroic period of functional typography, since it bore all the marks of that era's aesthetic legacy; simultaneously, it signalled the advent of a new and less rigorous trend.

Photomontage

The proliferation of photomontage 'as an artistic method' in the mid-1920's and its establishment till the late 1930's can be explained both artistically and socially. The demand for factual literature and art gave rise to the documentary film, 'truth-cinema', reportage-novel, photography and photomontage. Artistic technique using existing substances and a montage of elements stemmed from Constructivist influences but was not limited to them. Nowhere else in Europe, with the exception of Germany (mainly thanks to the work of J. Heartfield) and Poland, did photomontage gain such wide acceptance in the artistic realm. In post-revolutionary Russia it had, moreover, been assimilated by the mass-propaganda media. The effect of this was that in addition to photomontage close to the ideology of the new art, there also existed a naturalistic variant.

The forerunner of photomontage had been collage which had been discovered by Cubism and exploited by the Dadaists. Two of Malevich's oil paintings, *Still life with Mona Lisa* (1913) and *Lady of the bill-post* (1914), were typical examples of Cubist 'papiers collés'. In the years 1917–19 Rodchenko made attempts to combine materials with various surfaces, colours and consistencies. In the subsequent phase this Dadaist pastime turned into the so-called thematic collage. Individual letters, fragments of words from announcements, random patterns and ciphers, which in 'papiers collés' had formed a picture's spatial structure, now fell together on the basis of associations into statements and thoughts striking a blow, as was their author's intention, at the negative aspects of life. Biting and truculent 'thematic' collages (1922) bordering on the scandalous and formally akin to the works of Hausmann, Schwitters and Hannah Höch, found themselves on the threshold of photomontage in the strict sense. Against the back-drop of Mayakovsky's poem 'Pro Eto' (About This) Rodchenko created his first series of eleven photomontages, one of his best works. In them we do not find a literal illustration of the poetic text, but rather the artist's own commentary. Through the use of ambiguous metaphors Rodchenko wove his reflections on such concepts as love, happiness and the middle-class ideal in life. But in this anonymous collection of objects and people, anonymous photographs and reproductions taken from old prints, a personal motif appeared: the superimposed photographs of the poet and his lover Lili Brik. This totally unexpected incursion deepened the artistic fiction, transporting the reader into the realm of philosophical deliberation. Collage, photomontage, typomontage, photogram and photograph became elements ever more widely used in Rodchenko's creative pursuits. In 1924 he decided to take up photography himself, and this step was decisive for his future career as an experimental photographer and had an influence on his general artistic thinking. The photographic lens and photosensitive paper helped the artist to overturn stereotypes of perception as well as the conventional appearance of things.

In Lissitzky's creative pursuits painting imperceptibly flowed into photography and the related technique of photomechanics. 'Prouns', which in the view of researchers can be considered a stepping stone to architecture, to no less an extent bridged the gap leading to photographic imagination. It should be added that Lissitzky was one of the first to introduce large-scale photography to the architecture of exhibition arrangement. And what is more, he abandoned the principle of two dimensional displays in favour of montages of photograph-frescoes in space.

He was not much taken up with collage. Under the influence of personal contacts with Moholy-Nagy and the experiments of Man Ray he became interested in photography without actually using a camera. He was fascinated by the adventure of photographic substance itself: the improvised play of light on paper, the unexpected surprises of the darkroom, the astonishing artistry of images produced by piled and superimposed negatives. In this way he achieved a substitute for graphic art. Here are a few examples: the poster advertising 'Pelikan' ink (1924) came to life almost entirely in the darkroom out of objects left upon photosensitive paper. For the cover of a book by I. Selvinsky, *Poet's Notes* (1924), he used the simultaneous portrait of Hans Arp made earlier. A publication of the Vkhutemas Faculty of Architecture (1927) had a two-coloured cover featuring a hand and compass on millimetre-thin paper. This was a copy of a photograph of a self-portrait *Konstruktor* (1924), effected by combining a number of negatives superimposed on one another. The extraordinary expressiveness of the poster 'Russische Ausstellung' (1929), calling to mind the product of a surrealistic imagination, was also in part a mechanical creation produced by copying two negatives. This work is one of the world's major achievements in the field of poster art.

Gustav Klutsis owes his popularity throughout the world to a series of photomontage posters produced in the years 1930–3. Nevertheless, they were not on a par with the works of his experimental period, when the young Latvian painter had been in contact with Malevich, Lissitzky and Rodchenko. Before becoming a lecturer at the Vkhutemas Architecture Faculty (1924) he had previously conducted experiments with spatial forms, designed future audio-visual devices (1922), and been involved with photomontage. Under his first photocollage, *Dynamic City*, he had placed the following commentary: 'Voluminally spatial Suprematism+photomontage. The overthrow of non-objectivity and the birth of photomontage as an independent art-form.'

The artist's imagination and that of the entire *avant-garde* was fascinated by the personality of the leader of the Russian revolution, Lenin – by his extraordinary intellect and oratorical skills and the constructive nature of the idea which he both propagated and practised. The Revolution was associated with the romantic vision of a free intellect probing unknown and as yet unexplored reaches – and also with a powerful, organized energy source activating the purposeful pursuits of the collective.

The announcement of the Electrification Plan, the prelude to a sweeping programme of national industrialization, was favourably received. Lenin's statement: 'Communism means Soviet rule+electrification' is well known. Klutsis rose to the occasion with a photomontage (1920) which he planned to incorporate in a poster. A photograph of Lenin walking, coupled with an axonometric drawing, created the impression of infinite space. In order to honour the memory of Lenin, Klutsis, together with S. Senkin (Rodchenko contributed only one work), prepared a series of photomontages for a special publication. Today a rare museum piece, the work contained fourteen full-page, two-colour compositions, most of which were untitled. Hence it was called a 'photo-slogan-montage'. The clear-cut propaganda intention does not deprive these works of the traits of an artistic experiment. Its authors did not fill up the entire visual plane, as did Heartfield, for one. Space is approached in the painter's manner; as in Cubist pictures it is opposed to natural space. In addition to imposed photographs, fragments of other materials are also used, such as drawings, photographic film, drawn letters. Klutsis made use of a fragmentary drawing of a 'radio-orator' model. This form of auto-quotation, not used by anyone previously, caused a dissonance between mechanical material and the structure prepared by the artist himself. Senkin, by contrast, introduced a certain innovation. Instead of the block letter eagerly used by the Constructivists, he decided on typewritten letters. The authors' second commemorative photomontage work, 'Lenin i dyeti' (1924), was also characterized by a free approach to the topic, adapted to the level of the younger reader. It had nothing in common with the schematism to which Klutsis succumbed in his later period.

The photomontages of Telingater date from the 1930's. In 1934 he illustrated *The Year 1914*, a book by I. Feinberg on preparations for World War I, by the use of photomontages arranged as a visual narrative. Although the pictures abounded with naïve metaphors and banal symbolism, the work none the less attested to the continuation of a vital trend in Soviet art in the new and changed ideational climate of the 1930's.

The art of photomontage in the USSR developed under the wing of outstanding artistic schools. Mention has already been made of the inspiration which it drew from Constructivism. Another sphere of influence derived from the film aesthetics of the 'kinoki'[29] and their most widely acclaimed representative, Dziga Vertov. From these sources flowed the ideas of dynamic montage, abbreviated imagery and new concepts in form: the undermining of the unity of time and place, the principle of simultaneity, overlapping motifs, quotations, heightened realism of detail, and the expression of an object as caught by the camera.

Posters

The art of the revolution expressed itself most fully and dramatically in the graphics of the poster. How did this come about?

The social upheaval had liberated the energy of millions of people. Workers, peasants, illiterates inhabiting the vast expanses of the empire of the Tsar Nicholas were sucked into the whirlwind of historical events. In their villages they had been isolated from all material and spiritual culture. In a countryside dominated by patriarchal relations, peasants had been the victims of national persecution. The Bolsheviks were faced with a problem of prime importance, that of instilling a Communist awareness in broad segments of society, teaching it to understand the meaning and goals of the Revolution. It became necessary, therefore, to develop educational and propaganda activities by all possible means. It was soon discovered that 'agitprop' making use of pictures could play no less significant a role than spoken or written words. Pictures displayed in public places helped to transcend the language barrier which was extremely important in a land with a multi-national population. During the civil war and blockade, pictures outstripped and often replaced the press, the megaphone installed in a public square or the eloquence of the orator at mass-meetings. Various forms of 'agitation art' underwent a rapid and flourishing development. Mayakovsky called for 'all the sides, foreheads and bosoms of towns, stations and speeding trains' to be plastered with pictures. Trains featuring allegorical and symbolic scenes departed on long-distance runs heading for Turkestan, the Caucasus and the banks of the Don. Antiquated ships cruising the rivers became floating frescoes. Workers' holidays and folk festivals provided the occasion for mass spectacles. Squares became transformed into folk theatres. Soldiers, sailors and workers made up both audience and actors, as they acted out the storming of the old world. The backdrop for such shows were huge panels, bashfully hiding from view the classical façades of palaces. Agitprop pictures were transported by lorries in the parades and adorned the exteriors of trams.

Posters and wall decorations became street-corner narrators, and like illustrated newspapers they were meant both for viewing and reading. They were the forerunners of the contemporary 'bandes dessinées' (cartoon strips) – tales with a moral brought together to make a particular point or under a common title. 'The traditional book has been scattered in various directions, enlarged a hundred times, colouristically intensified and, in the form of a poster, displayed in the streets.' So said Lissitzky.

The early agitation poster was deeply rooted in spontaneous Russian culture; its godparents were the folk lubok and icon. Its character was also moulded to a considerable degree by the influence of the satirical graphics of the 1905 revolution. The icon, the most closely related model of 'popular' art, provided the repertoire of signs: the flat moulding of figures, conventional space, and the abstract effects of colours. The poster owes its freshness and authenticity of experience as well as its form of naïve realism to the lubok tradition, in which the anonymous artist gave vent to his longing for justice and good. The poster style of Rosta (Russian Telegraphic Agency), created by Mayakovsky, Cheremnykh, Lebedev, Kozlinsky and others, traced its lineage directly to the language of folk art. In his posters divided into quarters, Mayakovsky introduced object symbols and figures personifying various attitudes. The schematic drawing, subsequently duplicated by stencil, made it possible to recognize stereotype situations and characters. The force behind these posters lies in their talent for communication. The more expressive drawings and use of colour in Lebedev's posters, cut from linoleum, were an example of the development of the Cubist concept of the object linked to Russian tradition. The posters of D. Moor were related to the widespread folk sayings, proverbs and tales. The specific details were expanded by the folk imagination and transformed into a universal concept. Less synthetic, V. Deni was also in favour of a condensed, partially realistic and partially grotesque form. A mélange of Romanticism, descriptive Realism and the artistic achievements of the early twentieth century was characteristic of the agitation works of Mayakovsky, Lebedev, A. Lavinsky, V. Roskin, the Ukrainian innovative painter M. Boychuk and others. Its total effect was unique and has had an astonishing influence on international poster art up to the present time. Where should Lissitzky's poster 'Beat the Whites with the Red Wedge' be ranked in this context?

His works have become widely accepted only in our times, popularized by historians of modern art. When use was made of his creations for the benefit of the Red Army in 1919, it was a major event, clearly ahead of its time. But, strictly speaking, he was not alone. The Smolensk branch of Rosta was the origin of an anonymous poster bearing the slogan: 'What have you done for the front?' (1920). It, too, was built up from a combination of abstract motifs, which, however, were free of any semantic undertones. Well known were the attempts to harness painting of 'pure feeling' to architecture, urban decoration, theatre interiors, announcements, advertisements, etc. Among other examples might be cited an agitprop tram in a May Day Parade at Vitebsk ascribed to Malevich, an agitprop car and theatre interior at Orenburg designed by I. Kudriashev, a theatre curtain jointly created by Lissitzky and Malevich, and the practical pursuits of Unovis.[30] But it was Lissitzky's posters which showed the greatest possibility of enriching the artistic language and which went down in the history of the poster as an example of the synthesis of a functional aim and free and independent expression.

After war operations had ceased and the country's reconstruction had begun, visual agitation lost much of its initial impetus. Cultural matters and even commercial advertisements came to the fore. In this area Constructivism with its rationalist philosophy and principles of economy and purposefulness rendered an undeniable service. In collaboration with Mayakovsky who wrote the texts, Rodchenko became involved in advertising for department stores and enterprises, encompassing packaging, posters, bills, and even street advertisements and electric signs. Not being hampered in his endeavours in any way, Rodchenko was able to display a genuine sense of humour.

Certain advertising gimmicks have a universal power and influence. In Paris, Cassandre devised a comical character to advertise the apéritif Dubonnet – a character which amused the public for years. In Moscow, no less famous was an impish puppet-like creation extolling the virtues of a baby's dummy so outstanding that an infant would want to suck on it till the end of its days. Nevertheless, gags and jokes arose spontaneously in the atmosphere of an exceedingly colourful and vivid cultural life.

The theatre of 'attractions', eccentric and grotesque buffoonery featuring highly mechanical hand-propelled Constructivist devices, and the theatre of montage, portraying unexpected situations and phenomena, were the primary school for the artistic thinking of the brothers Stenberg. They had been led to the theatre via their constructive-spatial and spatial-colouristic studies, undertaken jointly with K. Medunetzky at the Constructivist Laboratory in 1919–20. They began by designing posters for Tairov's 'Kamernyj' theatre where they were employed as decorators. Their first film poster 'Glaza luibvi' (Eyes of Love), signed 'Sten', was designed in 1924. (They later signed themselves as '2 Stenberg 2'.) They always worked together until the tragic death of Georgy in 1933 in a car accident. Of the two, Georgy had displayed a talent for colour and creative innovation, whereas Vladimir had an inventor's mind, an engineering mentality and a well-developed spatial sense.

In this way they had been able to complement one another in their scenographic work and graphic pursuits. By contrast with Lissitzky and Rodchenko, the Stenbergs made use of photographs only on rare occasions. As orthodox Constructivists, they naturally considered mechanical procedures superior to manual operations, and lens optics superior to brush-strokes. But they were fully aware of the fact that existing printing facilities were insufficient to provide adequate reproduction of photographs in black-and-white, let alone in colour. Necessity, however, being the mother of invention, the brothers Stenberg came upon the idea of simulating the 'magical realism' of photography. In their graphic techniques they succeeded in achieving incredible mimetic effects. Incidentally, it might be mentioned that creative precision and technical perfection held for them the greatest fascination. Their work on posters developed in several stages. From film studios they received strips of film and only on rare occasions actual photographs. They would divide a selected film-frame into tiny squares and then, by using a primitive optical device, they transferred the image to the wall, enlarging it precisely square by square. They perfected this method by designing a special projector which made it possible to change the film-frame composition. And so, for example, they could move the image along the diagonal or shorten its perspective. Whenever they advertised a film starring a popular actor (e.g. Buster Keaton, Douglas Fairbanks) they strove towards maximum resemblance. But mimesis did not mean a mirror-like reflection. They coupled a three-dimensional, almost stereoscopic, illusion with a flat graphic form, thereby enhancing even more succinctly their 'magical realism' ('Zemlia', 1930). The skeletal framework of every poster was a dynamic montage reminiscent of film techniques by virtue of its rapidly changing frames, sets and camera angles. Generally their repertoire consisted of the following combinations: large and small-plan montage ('Namus', 1926, 'Smiertnyj nomer', 'Odinatzatyj', 1928), various perspective shots and foreshortenings ('Viesnoy', 1929, 'Cheloviek s kinoaparaton', 1929), silhouette and three-dimensional form ('Negro-Operetta', 1929), multiplication ('The General', 2nd version, 1929). They applied fracture treatment to subtitles ('The General', 1st version, 1929), and ring or step systems ('Robin Hood').

By the mid-1920's numerous graphic artists had become involved in film posters. The second exhibition of film posters (1926), which attracted works from as many as twenty-seven artists, was evidence of the great attraction of this genre. It was a place for comparing and contrasting various exhibition techniques and brought the Stenberg Brothers well-deserved recognition. N. Prusakov designed an original poster for the event. But fate was unkind to this undoubtedly talented artist, and, with the exception of a few minute fragments, his life's work remains virtually unknown. It is known that he belonged to the same artistic generation and circle as the Stenberg Brothers and Rodchenko and studied at Vkhutemas for some time. He jointly exhibited his works at the Obmokhu (Young Constructivist Artists) exhibition in 1919 and 1921, at the Discussion Exhibition of the Association of Revolutionary Art Activists (1924), and at the International Press Exhibition at Cologne (1928). In his article 'Art and Pangeometry'[31] Lissitzky discussed the initial kinetic experiments of Russian Constructivists, citing by way of example Tatlin, Gabo and Prusakov who in 1921 had constructed a moving bas-relief. Later he became involved in exhibition arrangement and scenography. For a time he lectured at Moscow's Institute of Applied Art. His graphic endeavours date primarily from the period 1924–32. Some of his posters were jointly designed with G. Borisov and L. Naumov. Prusakov made use of various graphic techniques which he brought together, not always successfully, and various conventions including the grotesque and caricature. His movement from one style to the next without any logical motivation and consistency had a negative effect on his total creative output. In addition to posters of extremely forceful expression and original artistic construction, he also signed his name to embarrassingly banal works at the same time. None the less, Prusakov possessed a critical mind. He conducted an intellectual search, even though he went astray in selecting a road to follow. His poster for the film 'Chiny i liudi' (1929), an intriguing multi-strata photograph in the photo-typo-montage vein, was a precursor of what a score of years later would be accepted in graphics as an achievement of contemporary art. Not having ready-made screens at his disposal, he broke down his surface by means of hand-drawn screens, thereby achieving an optical vibration of the texture. He also tried his hand at multiplication in a documentary film 'Vierkhom na kholtie', independently of Vertov's pursuits in this area.

The principle of montage was also implemented by those members of the *avant-garde* movement who only sporadically came out with a poster, e.g. E. Semionova's posters for 'Sinaya Bluza', a workers' theatre.

In the 1930's the Constructivist tendency was beginning to exhaust itself, although this was a gradual process. Klutsis was still at work on propaganda and production posters. B. Klinch made use of photomontage and A. Deyneka, aligned with a different artistic school, continued to draw his inspiration from the best traditions of the revolutionary poster.

Conclusion

In creating the culture of a new society, graphic art occupied no minor position. It entered the domain of daily existence, forming the visual framework of the mass media and all the printed matter with which man is surrounded. Owing to its universality and general comprehensibility it exerted an influence on the moulding of current notions of art and of the beauty of common objects. As a harbinger of things to come, it proposed new and as yet untried aesthetic patterns. Although by nature it was basically a plebeian art-form, it did not 'talk down' to its audience. Instead, it strove to couple the principle of egalitarianism with the ideas of the *avant-garde*.

Mounting interest in the country's own revolutionary tradition was responsible for the fact that this wealth of artistic experience was rediscovered in the mid-1950's, and lessons for the present period were drawn from it. At the inauguration of the first post-war exhibition of Rodchenko's works in Moscow (1957), an address full of historical reflections was delivered by the poet S. Kirsanov, one of the participants in the *Lef* group. Among other things he said the following: 'Mention is often made of the asceticism of the artistic left wing ... This was an asceticism of simplicity, a straight-lined asceticism which brought an end to ornamentation. Our departure from asceticism has led to the proliferation of middle-class art on a large scale. When I gaze upon the posters and covers of Rodchenko, they seem to be the beginning of something which was never continued. It is sad that middle-class art, as personified by thousands of pink lampshades glowing in the windows of new flats, has managed to nip these early germs in the bud.'[32] A complicated amalgam of customs, social, cultural and even political factors had been responsible for such a state of affairs. But this is a subject in itself which has yet to receive scholarly treatment. There are many signs attesting to changes in the consciousness of the new generation of artists, to their desire to continue under present-day conditions the ideals of the artistic pioneers.

Mass media technology today puts at the disposal of the graphic designer much richer, productive and above all more influential means of visual communication than those that were used half a century ago by Mayakovsky, Lissitzky, the Stenberg brothers or Rodchenko. However, those seemingly primitive activities and forms of artistic expression still retain their full intellectual and aesthetic purposefulness. Their lasting values, studied critically but eagerly by the young, guarantee the at one time disturbed link between the romantic and revolutionary past and the present day. Experiments in the field of Soviet posters, as demonstrated, for example, at the International Poster Biennale in Warsaw, as well as the interesting graphic solutions to be found in illustrated magazines (especially popular-scientific ones), and in books for children, and the development of a new branch of graphic design, connected with the identification of an industrial product through advertising – all these prove that the broken link has been established anew.

The Constructivist ethos, however, is not limited by national frontiers; it is the cultural possession of all mankind. Even though it represents an earlier chapter in history, its presence is felt in numerous areas of contemporary art. To our troubled and conflict-ridden world, it introduces elements of equilibrium, order and simplicity.

Notes

[1] Higher Technical-Artistic Studios (1920–30), the school established in Moscow after the liquidation of the Tsarist academies. It gathered several outstanding artists and, like the Bauhaus group, became famous for its new teaching methods.

[2] From the archives of A. Rodchenko.

[3] A Russian variant of an artistic trend known in western Europe as 'Art Nouveau', 'Jugendstil', 'Secession', etc.

[4] An abbreviated form of the name of a group of late 19th-century painters. At the beginning of this century the Pyredvizhnikovs' realistic traditions hampered the development of avant-garde art.

[5] Both quotations from the 'Sovietskoye Iskusstvo za 15 let' (Soviet art in Fifteen Years), Moscow, 1933.

[6] The Productivists Group, a radical wing of the Russian avant-garde which argued against the need to create art serving social ideological ends.

[7] The community of Futurist poets set up by David Burluk in 1911. It was called Gileya (Hylaea) after the ancient Greek colony on the Dnieper river.

[8] An artistic group set up at the beginning of 1911 whose members included, among others, Larionov, Goncharova, Malevich and Tatlin.

[9] An artistic group set up in St Petersburg in 1910; it was founded by the brothers Burluk, Rozanova and Matyushin.

[10] The manifesto proclaimed in 1912 was signed by D. Burluk, A. Kruchyonykh, V. Mayakovsky and V. Khlebnikov.

[11] V. Khlebnikov, A. Khruchyonykh. 'Bukva kak takovaya', 1913. *Sobranye proizvedenyi*. Volume V, 1933.

[12] 'Troye', 1913.

[13] 'The typography of typography', an article cited later in the text.

[14] A folk picture made as a woodcut or copper engraving.

[15] From the file of N. Leporskaya, the artist's wife.

[16] *Merz*, No.4, 1923.

[17] El Lissitzky, Dresden, 1967.

[18] A literary monthly edited by V. Mayakovsky (1923–5), and the name of a literary-and-artistic group.

[19] Novoye o Mayakovskom, Moscow, 1958.

[20] The Institute of Artistic Culture, art and research centre set up in 1920; Kandinsky was one of its founders. Its members occupied themselves, among other things, with the so-called objective analysis of painting.

[21] From the archives of A. Rodchenko.

[22] From the open letter 'Roads to Contemporary Photography', *Novi Lef*, No.9, 1928.

[23] The unpublished typescript is preserved in the Mayakovsky Museum in Moscow.

[24] *op.cit.,* p.239 (French edition).

[25] Fotomontazh kak novyj vid agitacyonnovo iskusstva. Joint publications entitled: Klassovaya borba na frontye prostranstviennikh iskusstv. Moscow, 1931.

[26] Published in the Polish magazine *Fotografia*, No.11, 1970.

[27] M. Ilyin, Vesniny. Moscow, 1960.

[28] The Union of Communist Youth.

[29] The Kino-oko (The Film-Eye) film school. Its chief ideologist, Dziga Vertov, advocated the need to register life as it is.

[30] An artistic group which grew up at Vitebsk.

[31] *Kunst und Pangeometrie*, Europa Almanach, Potsdam, 1925.

[32] *Sovetskoye Photo*, No.2, 1962

Signboards for a clothing store
painted by V. Stiepanov, *c.*1910
Municipal Museum, Leningrad

Natalia Goncharova:
Cover for a book by Kruchyonykh
and Khlebnikov, 1912

Mikhail Larionov:
Page from Kruchyonykh's poem
'Pomada', 1913

Kasimir Malevich:
Cover design for poems by
Khlebnikov, Kruchyonykh and Guro, 1913

Vladimir Mayakovsky:
Cover design, 1913

Pavel Filonov:
Double-spread from Khlebnikov's book
'Wooden gods', 1914

Olga Rozanova:
Cover for Khlebnikov's and
Kruchyonykh's book 'Telile', 1914

Poster for Futurist meeting,
Kazan, 1914

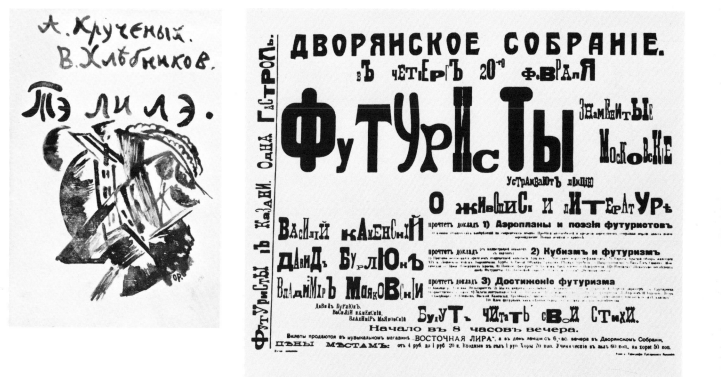

Vasily Seletzky:
'On the eve of the World Social
Revolution',
Poster, Moscow, March 1917

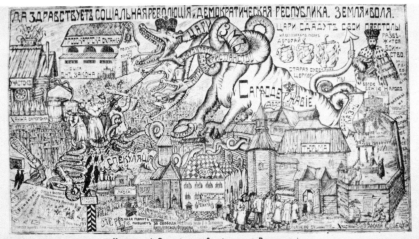

Victor Deni:
'Capital', Poster, 1919

Mikhail Cheremnykh (right):
'All to help Donbass', Rosta window,
1920

Vladimir Kozlinsky:
Rosta poster (part) from Petrograd,
Linoleum print, 1920/21

Vladimir Kozlinsky:
'Ignoring three years' endeavours
of our enemies',
Poster, 1920

El Lissitzky:
'Beat the Whites with the Red Wedge',
Poster, Vitebsk 1919

Kasimir Malevich:
'What have you done for the front?'
Rosta window, Smolensk 1919

А что ты сделал для фронта?
Отдай последнее тем, кто умирает, защищая тебя.

СМОЛРОСТА.

РАБОТАТЬ НАДО ВИНТОВКА-РЯДОМ

ПЕТЕРБУРГ РОСТА

Vladimir Lebedev:
Rosta window, Petrograd 1920

Vladimir Lebedev (right):
'Old man Prov. . .'
Rosta poster, Petrograd 1920

Vladimir Lebedev:
New bourgeoisie
Rosta poster, Petrograd 1921

Vladimir Roskin:
'In America you have your fill . . .'
Rosta window (fragment), 1920

1. В АМЕРИКЕ СЫТНО

ВМЕСТО РАЗВЕРСТКИ-НАЛОГ!

РАЗВЕРСТКА ОТЯГЧАЛА КРЕСТЬЯН ЧРЕЗМЕРНО ЭТО, ТОВАРИЩИ ВЕРНО.

НО ЕСЛИ Б ХЛЕБА МЫ НЕ РАЗВЕРСТАЛИ, ЧЕМ-БЫ АРМИЮ КОРМИТЬ СТАЛИ?

— А БЕЗ АРМИИ СОЖРАЛ БЫ ПОМЕЩИК КРЕСТЬЯН ВМЕСТЕ С ПРОДУКТАМИ И С БАЗАРАМИ.

СЕЙЧАС ОПАСНОСТИ НА ФРОНТАХ НЕТ.

РАБОЧЕ-КРЕСТЬЯНСКОЕ ПРАВИТЕЛЬСТВО ИЗДАЛО ДЕКРЕТ РАЗВЕРСТКА ОТМЕНЯЕТСЯ!

ОБОРАЧИВАЙ И ОБМЕНИВАЙ, КРЕСТЬЯНИН, МУКУ, МЯСО И ЯЙЦА.

Vladimir Mayakovsky:
Rosta window (detail), 1921

Varvara Stepanova:
Poster for 'Death of Tarelkin'
(produced by Meyerhold), 1922

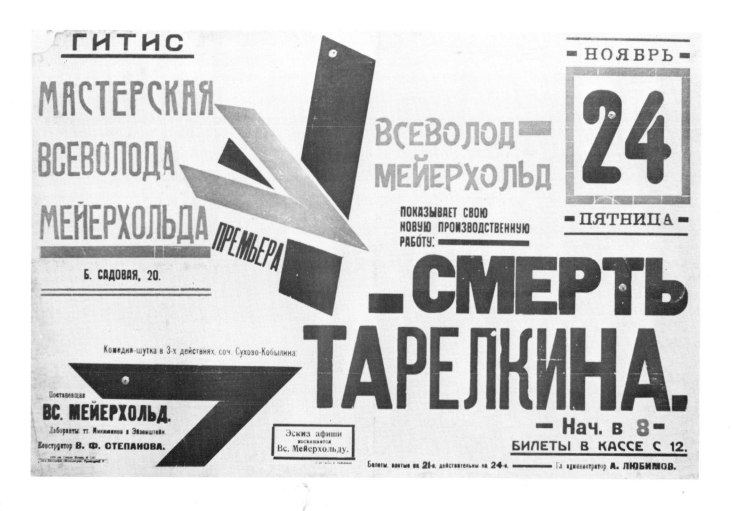

Georgy and Vladimir Stenberg:
Poster for Sokolov's puppet show, 1923

Yuriy Annenkov:
Theatre poster for the play 'The revolt
of the machines', 1924

Alexander Rodchenko:
'The Press is our weapon',
Poster, 1923

Alexander Rodchenko:
Poster for the International Press
Exhibition, Cologne 1928

Alexander Rodchenko:
Poster for Vertov's film 'Cinema Eye',
1924

Anton Lavinsky:
Poster for the film
'The Battleship Potemkin',
1926

Gustav Klutsis:
Leaflet advocating professional
training for women-workers, 1927

Grigory Borisov and Nikolay Prusakov:
Film poster for
'The house at Trubna Street', 1928

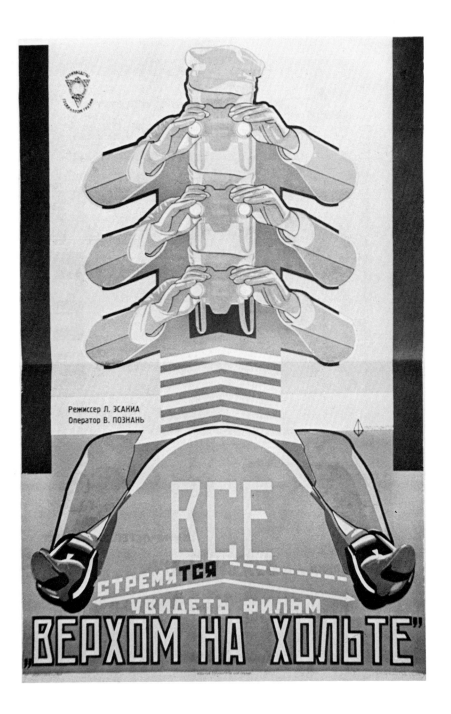

Nikolay Prusakov:
Film poster for 'Verkhom na kholtye',
1928

Georgy and Vladimir Stenberg:
Film poster for Buster Keaton's
'The General', 1928

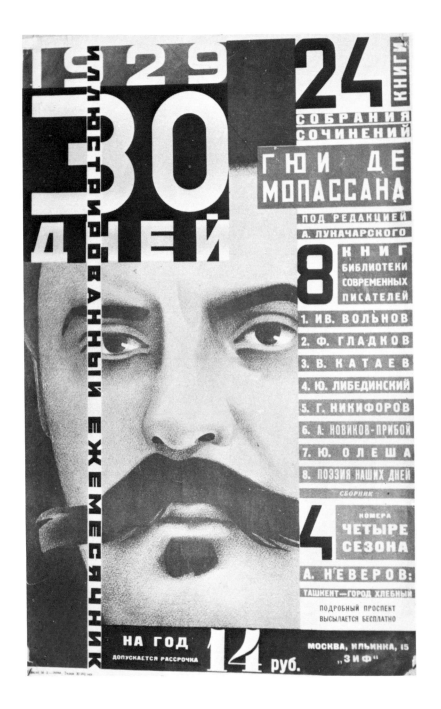

Georgy and Vladimir Stenberg:
Poster advertising the literary
monthly '30 days', 1929

Nikolay Prusakov:
Film poster for 'A Strange Woman', 1929

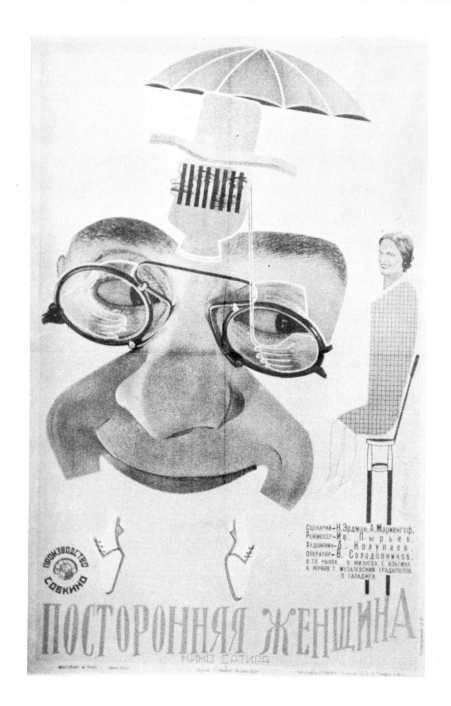

Nikolay Prusakov:
Film poster for 'Tchiny i liudi'
(People and bureaucracy), 1929

Georgy and Vladimir Stenberg:
Poster for 'Negro-Operetta', 1929

Georgy and Vladimir Stenberg:
Film poster for 'Fragment of Empire',
1929

Georgy and Vladimir Stenberg:
Film poster for 'Spring', 1929

Georgy and Vladimir Stenberg:
Poster
'To the fallow ground', 1928

El Lissitzky:
Russian exhibition, Zürich,
Poster, 1929

COLLEGE LIBRARY
COLLEGE OF TECHNOLOGY
CARNARVON ROAD
SOUTHEND-ON-SEA, ESSEX

Gustav Klutsis:
The Coal Miner's poster, 1930

Gustav Klutsis:
Poster for an Anti-imperialist
Exhibition, 1931

Packaging for 'Mosselprom' cigarettes,
c.1925

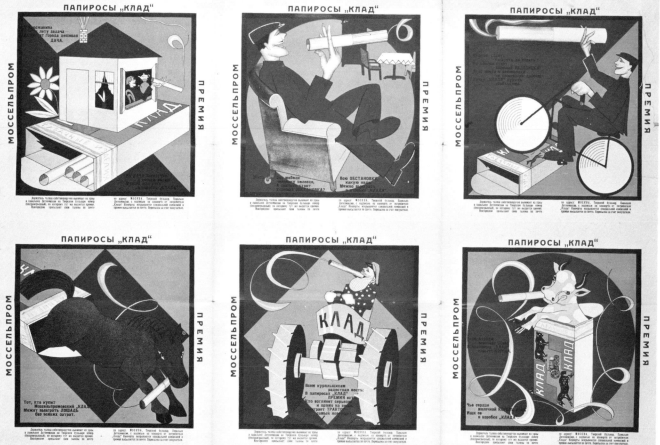

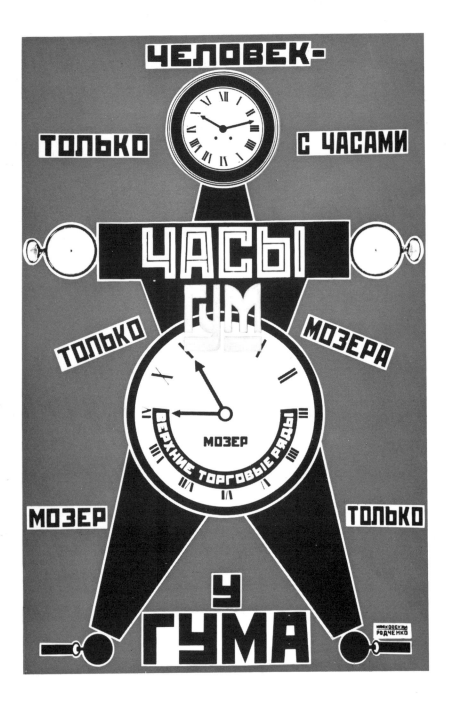

Alexander Rodchenko:
Advertisement for the 'GUM'
Department Store:
copy by Mayakovsky, 1923

Alexander Rodchenko:
Poster advertising baby's dummy:
copy by Mayakovsky, 1923

Alexander Rodchenko:
One of the first advertisements for the
'GUM' Department Store: copy by
Mayakovsky. Appeared in 'Izvestya',
1923

Vladimir Mayakovsky (right):
Poster for Resinotrest, 1924

ДОЖДИК ДОЖДЬ ВПУСТУЮ ЛЬЕШЬ
Я НЕ ВЫЙДУ БЕЗ ГАЛОШ.
С ПОМОЩЬЮ РЕЗИНОТРЕСТА
МНЕ ВЕЗДЕ СУХОЕ МЕСТО.
ПРОДАЖА ВЕЗДЕ

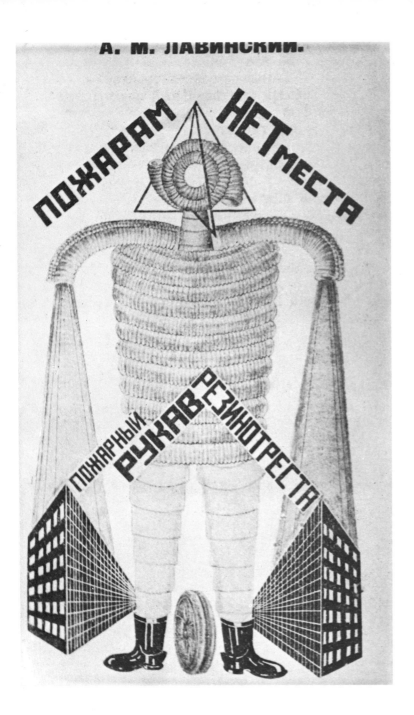

Anton Lavinsky:
Advertisement layout for Resinotrest,
1924

Alexander Rodchenko:
Advertisement layout for
the 'GUM' Department Store:
copy by Mayakovsky, 1923

Alexander Rodchenko:
Design for a kiosk, 1919

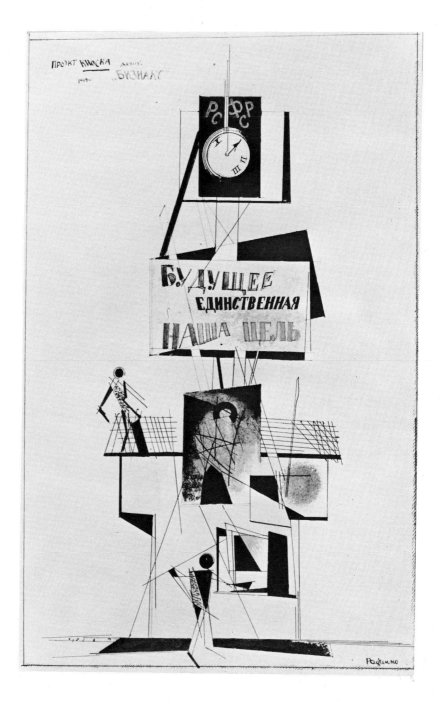

Agitprop tram in Vitebsk
designed by Kasimir Malevich, 1918

Propaganda ship 'Red Star', 1919

Propaganda train 'V. I. Lenin', 1920

S. Tikchonov:
Propaganda train 'Red Kozak', 1920

Gustav Klutsis:
'Sport', Photomontage, 1922

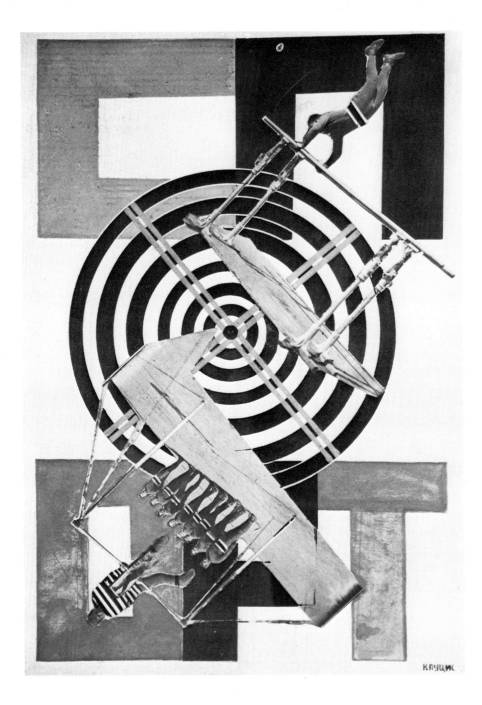

Alexander Rodchenko:
'The crisis', Photomontage, 1923

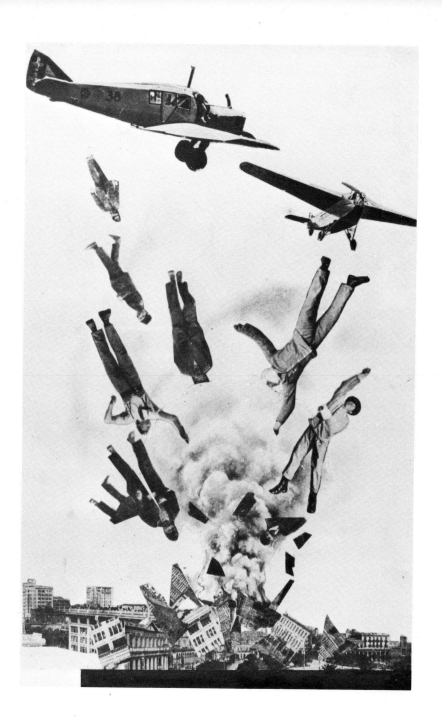

Alexander Rodchenko:
Photomontage for Mayakovsky's poem
'About this', 1923

Sergey Senkin (right):
Photomontage for 'Children and Lenin',
1924

Sergey Senkin:
Photomontage for a special edition of
'Molodaya gwardya' (To Lenin), 1924

Gustav Klutsis:
Photomontage for a special edition of
'Molodaya gwardya' (To Lenin), 1924

Gustav Klutsis:
Photomontage for a special edition of
'Molodaya gwardya' (To Lenin), 1924

Gustav Klutsis:
Photomontage for Mayakovsky's poem
'Lenin', 1925

Solomon Telingater:
Photomontage for I. Feinberg's book
'The Year 1914', 1934

Solomon Telingater:
Photomontage for I. Feinberg's
book 'The Year 1914', 1934

Lubov Popova:
Cover design, 1921

Anton Lavinsky:
Cover design for an anthology
by Mayakovsky '13 years' work', 1922

El Lissitzky:
Cover design for 'Veshch', 1922

Alexander Vesnin:
Cover for the magazine 'Architecture',
1923

Alexander Rodchenko:
Cover design for the magazine 'Lef',
1923

Alexander Rodchenko:
Cover design (back and front)
for Mayakovsky's poems, 1923

Vladimir Favorsky:
Cover for the magazine 'Makovets',
wood-engraving, 1923

Lubov Popova:
Cover design for a fashion magazine,
1924

Alexander Rodchenko:
Standard cover design for a series of
detective stories (allowing for variable
elements), 1924

Alexander Rodchenko:
Cover design for a detective story,
based on the design opposite, 1924

Grigory Miller:
Advertisement for a foreign language
school, 1924

Galina and Olga Chichagova:
Page from children's book
'How people travel', 1925

El Lissitzky (left):
Cover design
for 'The isms of art', 1924

Nikolay Suetin:
Cover design
for the magazine 'Kino', 1925

КИНО
ЖУРНАЛ
А.Р.К.

1925   № 2

МОСКВА

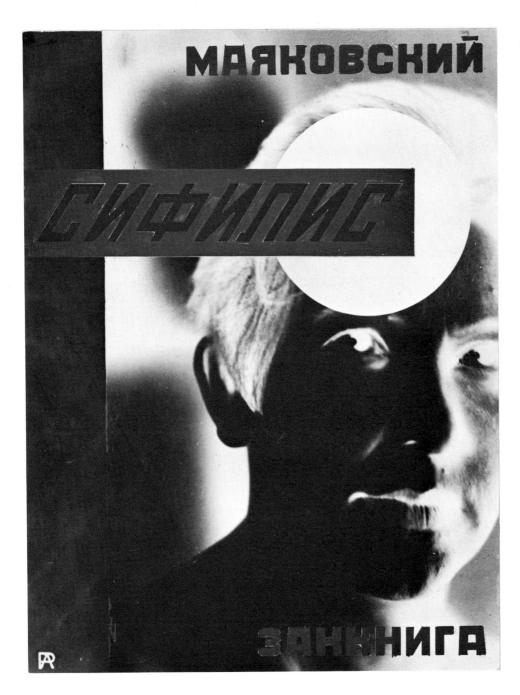

Alexander Rodchenko:
Cover design for Mayakovsky's poem
'Syfilis', 1926

El Lissitzky:
Cover design for 'Arkhitektura
Vkhutemas', 1927

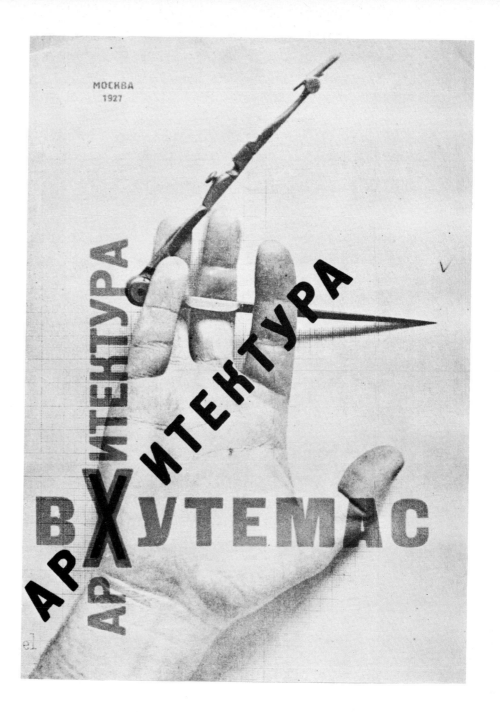

Alexander Rodchenko:
Cover for the magazine 'Novi Lef', No.3,
1927

Solomon Telingater:
Cover design, 1927

Solomon Telingater:
Cover design, 1929

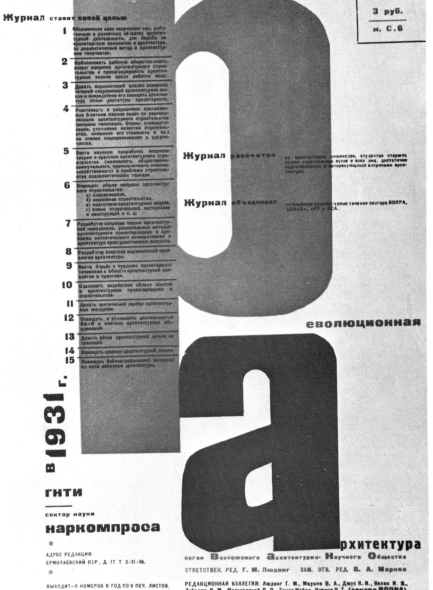

Solomon Telingater:
Cover design for the magazine
'Revolutsyonnaya Arkhitektura', 1927

Nikolay Sedelnikov:
Cover design for a typography
magazine, 1933

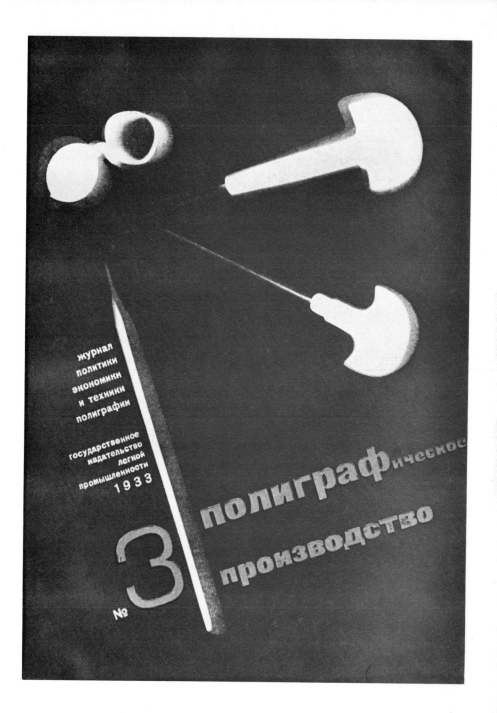

Vladimir Mayakovsky:
Series of drawings for comic-strip
'A story of the deserter', 1921

Vladimir Krinsky;
Newspaper design, 1922

Alexei Gan:
Layout for a magazine, c.1923

Alexander Rodchenko:
Title page for magazine 'Lef', 1923

Alexander Rodchenko:
Page from 'Lef', No.4, 1923

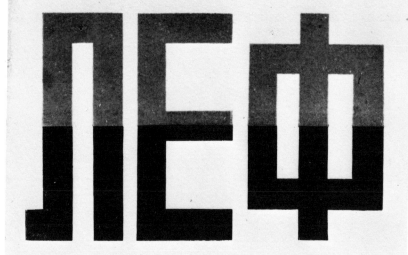

Alexander Rodchenko:
Film-title for Dziga Vertov's documentary
'Truth Cinema', 1924

Galina and Olga Chichagova:
Double-spread from a children's book
'To the children about newspapers',
1924

Утром чуть свет в редакцию прибегают мальчишки:
Каждый хватает себе пачку под мышку
И бежит, чтоб скорей разнесть ее.

БЕГУТ И ▬▬▬

КРИЧАТ ▬▬▬

▬▬▬

ГАЗЕТН КИОСК
ПРАВДА
Известия
1 ГОС.
КИНО-
ГОСИЗДАТ
— МОСКВА
ПЕТРОГРАД
НОВЫЕ КНИГИ.
ГОСИЗДАТ.
2-ой ГОСЦИРК
КИНО
ФОТ. № 7.

ИЗВЕСТИЯ!
ИЗВЕСТИЯ!

Чтоб попала газета во все места,
Развозят ее аэропланы, поезда,
И везде газету поджидают,
На Волге, в Крыму, на Алтае.

Galina and Olga Chichagova:
Page from a children's book
'Chaplin's travels', 1924

Galina and Olga Chichagova:
Page from a children's book
'To the children about newspapers',
1924

Помимо известий из Франции и Китая,

В газету и московские новости поступают:

ЕДИНСТВЕННЫЕ В МИРЕ
АТЛЕТЫ — СИЛАЧИ:

ПОДБРАСЫВАЮТ ГИРИ,
КАК ДЕТСКИЕ МЯЧИ.

Vladimir Lebedev:
Illustration for a children's book
'Circus', 1925

Vladimir and Georgy Stenberg:
Layout for the newspaper 'Izvestya',
Project, 1927

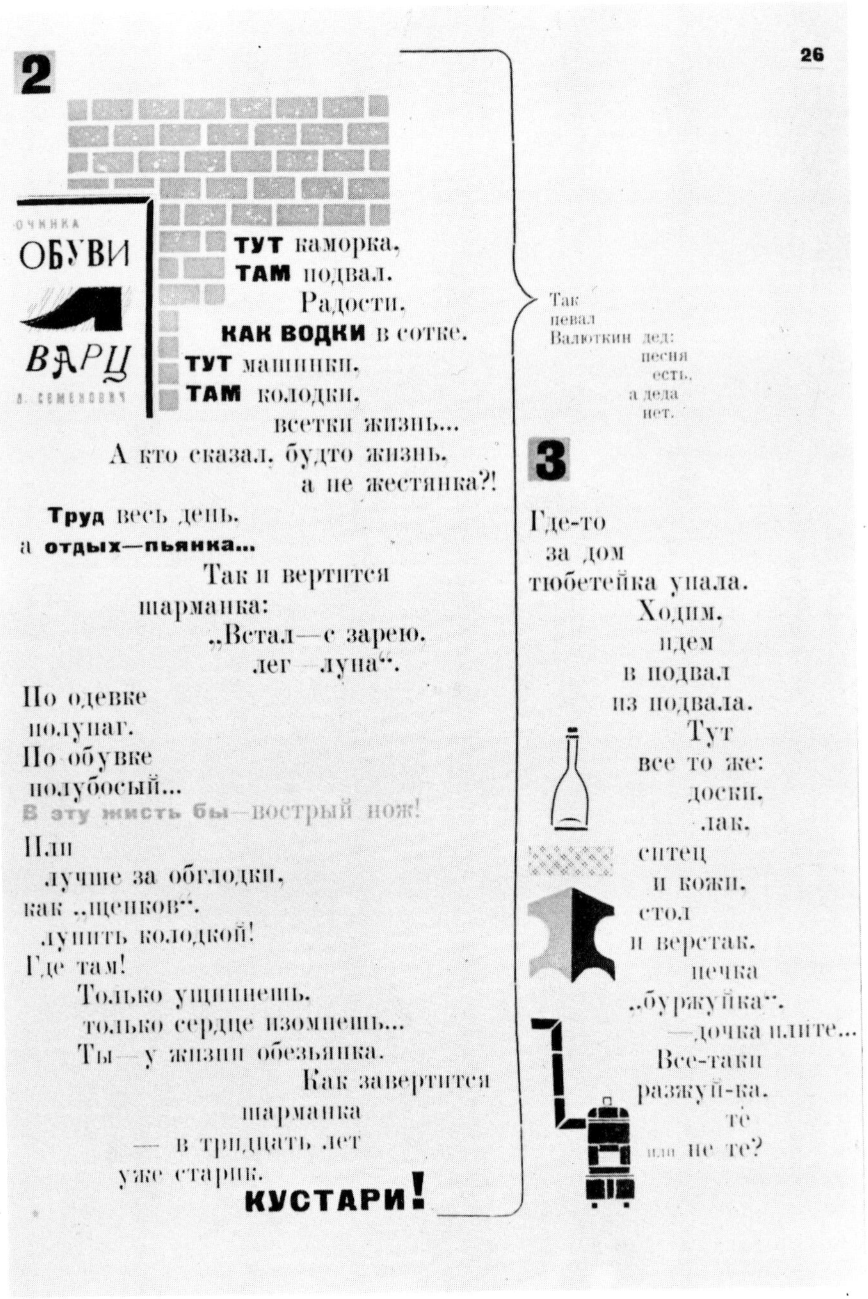

Solomon Telingater:
Page from A. Bezymiensky's book
'Komsomolya', 1928

2

ОБУВИ

ВАРЦ

ТУТ каморка,
ТАМ подвал.
Радости,
КАК ВОДКИ в сотке.
ТУТ машинки,
ТАМ колодки.
всетки жизнь...
А кто сказал, будто жизнь,
а не жестянка?!

Труд весь день,
а **отдых—пьянка...**
Так и вертится
шарманка:
„Встал—с зарею,
лег луна".

По одевке
полунаг,
По обувке
полубосый...
В эту жисть бы— вострый нож!

Или
лучше за обглодки,
как „щенков",
лупить колодкой!
Где там!
Только ущипнешь,
только сердце изомнешь...
Ты — у жизни обезьянка,
Как завертится
шарманка
— в тридцать лет
уже старик.
КУСТАРИ!

Так
певал
Валюткин дед:
песня
есть,
а деда
нет.

3

Где-то
за дом
тюбетейка упала.
Ходим,
идем
в подвал
из подвала.
Тут
все то же:
доски,
лак,
ситец
и кожи,
стол
и верстак.
печка
„буржуйка".
— дочка и лите...
Все-таки
разжуй-ка,
те
или не те?

El Lissitzky:
Double-spread from Mayakovsky's
'For reading out loud', 1929

СКАЗКА о КРАСНОЙ ШАПОЧКЕ

Жил да был на свете кадет,
В красную шапочку кадет был одет.
Кроме этой шапочки, доставшейся кадету,
ни черта в нем красного не было и нету.
Услышит кадет — революция где-то
шапочка сейчас-же на голове кадета.
Жили припеваючи за кадетом кадет
и отец кадета, и кадетов дед.

Поднялся однажды пребольшущий ветер —
в клочья шапченку изорвал на кадете.

И остался он черный, а видевшие это,
волки революции сцапали кадета.

Известно какая у волков диэта:
вместе с манжетами сожрали кадета.

Когда будете делать политику, дети,
не забудьте сказочку об этом кадете.

КАДЕТ

КУМА

ЛЮБОВЬ

К ЛОШАДЯМ

СОЛНЦЕ

Solomon Telingater:
Jacket for S. Kirsanov's novels, 1930

Alexander Rodchenko:
Three-dimensional illustration for
S. Tretiakov's children's book
'Samozveri', 1930

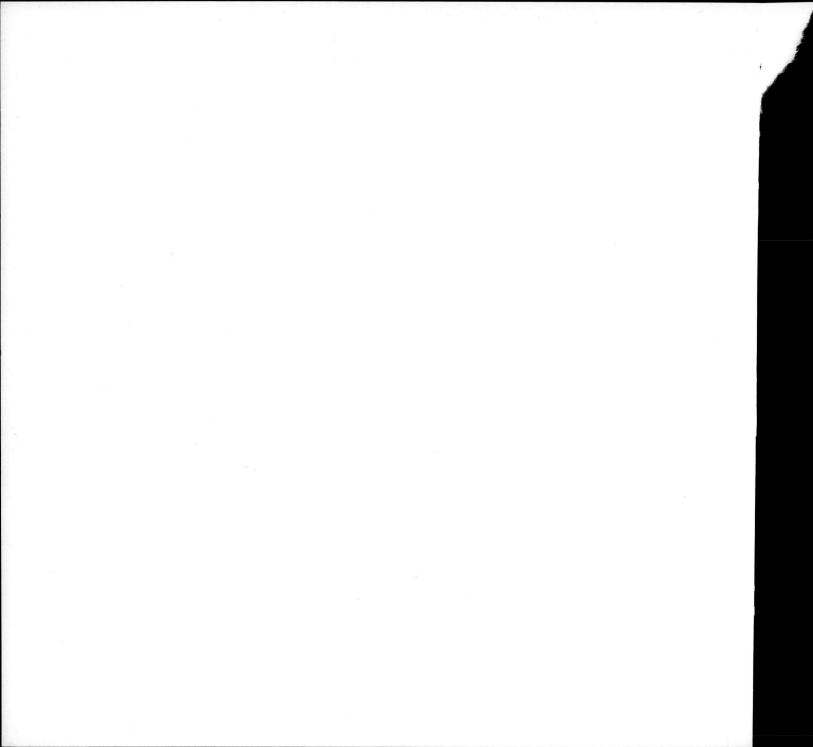

G. Stenberg (left) with I. Gerasimovich
in the studio of the Stenberg brothers

Biographical notes

Annenkov, Yury
born 1890

Studied law as well as drawing and painting. During the period 1911–13, stayed in Paris. Back in Russia he started to practise painting, designed book illustrations and stage settings. Among others, he illustrated A. Blok's poem 'The Twelve' (1918), and made a series of portraits of outstanding writers and artists. He was one of the authors of a huge street show reproducing 'The Storming of the Winter Palace' (Petrograd 1920). In 1927 emigrated from the Soviet Union.

Cheremnykh, Mikhail
1890–1962

Studied medicine and painting in Moscow. Organized the posters workshop attached to the Russian Telegraphic Agency (Rosta Windows), and was one of the foremost poster-makers of the period of the Civil War. His cartoons were printed in several newspapers, mainly in the *Krokodil* (The Crocodile) satirical magazine. Lectured on graphic art at the Moscow Institute of Art and educated several generations of poster-artists.

Chichagova, Galina
1891–1967
Chichagova, Olga
1892–1956

Two daughters of a Russian architect. They received a thorough education at home. For a certain time attended the Vkhutemas. Together with a poet, N. Smirnov, they formed a team designing children's books (1923). Their designs were shown at the First Polemical Exhibition (1921) together with works by members of the First Constructivists Working Group headed by Rodchenko. When at the Vkhutemas, the Chichagov sisters wrote a scenario and designed costumes for a mime performance 'Attending Passions' which they themselves staged in 1921. They also designed exhibition arrangements in co-operation with Lissitzky but then parted with him as a result of a difference in opinion. The two sisters jointy designed interiors for the Protection of Maternity Museum (1932).

Deni (Denisov), Victor
1893–1946

His first drawings appeared in newspapers in 1913. From 1921 he regularly contributed cartoons to *Pravda*. One of the foremost poster-artists of the period of the Civil War.

Favorsky, Vladimir
1886–1946

Studied art in Moscow and in Munich. Practised wood engraving, stage design and painting. Was rector of the Vkhutemas (1923–5) and professor of its Graphic Art Department. Published several theoretical studies concerning composition, book design, typography and lettering. He was awarded the Grand Prix at the Art Déco exhibition in Paris (1925), and at the World Exhibition (Paris 1937), and was granted the Special Prize at the International Wood Engraving Exhibition (Warsaw 1933). His wood engravings illustrated numerous classics of Russian and world literature, as well as covers of several other books and periodicals.

Filonov, Pavel
1883–1941

Studied art in Petrograd. Was member of the 'Union of Youth' (1910). Designed settings for the tragedy *Vladimir Mayakovsky* (1913). In the years 1914–15 he formulated the foundations of his own theory of painting and, together with his pupils, applied the so-called analytical method. He headed the general theoretical section of the State Institute of Artistic Culture (Ginkhuk 1923). Practised painting and book design. Illustrated several futuristic poems.

Gan, Alexei
1893–1939/40?

Practised applied graphic art, photography and design. Was art director of the periodical *Sovremiennaya Arkhitektura* (Contemporary Architecture) and member of the 'OSA' group of architects. His works were exhibited, among others, at the First Polemical Exhibition of Revolutionary Art (Moscow 1924), the First Film Posters Exhibition (Moscow 1925), and the First Exhibition of Graphic Art (Moscow 1926). He participated in the organization of the First Exhibition of Modern Architecture (Moscow 1927) and was one of the founders of the 'Oktiabr' (October) artists association (1928).

Goncharova, Natalia
1881–1962

Studied art in Moscow. She exhibited her works, among others, together with the 'Jack of Diamonds' group (Moscow 1910), the 'Union of Youth' (Petrograd 1910) and 'Der Blaue Reiter' (Munich 1912). Together with her husband, M. Larionov, she studied Russian folk art and icon painting. She illustrated futuristic poems. In 1915 Goncharova left Russia and settled in Paris.

Klutsis, Gustav
1895–1944

Started to study art in Riga. Actively participated in the October Revolution in Russia, including taking part in the memorable storming of the Winter Palace. Served in the Red Army and at the same time carried out visual propaganda. After the end of the Civil War, Klutsis continued his studies at the Vkhutemas and was then appointed professor of its Architecture Department and headed its Colour Study Group. He carried out a search for new applications of photography in conjunction with painting and graphic art. He contributed a great deal to the development of the photomontage technique as applied in poster art. Klutsis's *avant-garde* ideas found their expression in his approach towards space and movement in the work of art, most clearly revealed in his architectural projects expressing the dynamics of big cities ('The Dynamic City', 1919). He designed a series of spatial compositions with a practical application as a means of communication; these were the so-called radio-orators made on the occasion of the Fourth Congress of the Comintern (1922). His new ideas have contributed to the development of typography.

Kozlinsky, Vladimir
1889–1967

One of the founders of the propaganda posters workshop, the Petrograd branch of Rosta (1920). He was one of the authors of a monumental decoration of Petrograd (1918). His linoleum prints illustrated the album devoted to the 'Heroes and Victims of the Revolution' with texts by V. Mayakovsky (1919). Contributed drawings to several newspapers and made numerous graphic works. He was professor at the Moscow Institute of Art and Industrial Design.

Krinsky, Vladimir
1890–1971

Studied architecture. A co-founder of a group of painters, sculptors and architects (Zhivskulptarch, 1919) who rejected traditional artistic and architectural ideas, striving towards a new synthesis of the arts. He was a member of the teaching staff of the Vkhutemas at which he headed the Space Composition Study Group. He put forward his original ideas in a text-book designed for students. Was one of the founders of the 'Asnova' artists association (The Association of New Architects) set up in 1923. Together with N. Ladovsky he designed the first experimental 'communal houses' (1920). He designed an urban and engineering complex near the Moscow river. Apart from architecture, Krinsky also occupied himself with graphic art. His works were reprinted in foreign art publications, including the German 'A bis Z' (1930–1).

Larionov, Mikhail
1881–1964

Studied art in Moscow. His works were exhibited, with others, at the 'World of Art' (1911) and the 'Union of Youth' (1911) exhibitions. He was a co-founder of the 'Donkey's Tail' group (1912). His early paintings reveal his fascination with Russian folk painting and primitive art in general. In 1911 he started to paint abstract works known as 'Rayonist paintings'. He also made numerous drawings and illustrated poems by Futurists, e.g. Mayakovsky's 'The Sun' (1923). Left Russia in 1914. Husband of Natalia Goncharova.

Lavinsky, Anton
1893–1968

Headed the Sculpture Department of the Vkhutemas. Was closely linked with the *Lef* group and was a member of the Inkhuk. Made propaganda posters for the Moscow branch of Rosta Windows, as well as advertisements. Designed settings for the 'Mystery-Bouffe' (1921), experimental futuristic architectural projects (e.g., 'A sunny town', 'A house on legs'), kiosks, and other small architectural forms.

Lebedev, Vladımır
1891–1964

For a short time attended the Tsarist Academy of Art. His early drawings soon started to appear in newspapers. In the years 1918–21 lectured at the Independent Art Studios in Petrograd. The whole of his creative work was closely linked with this town. He was an expert on folk art, the elements of which he applied in his own works. Together with Kozlinsky, he headed the Petrograd branch of Rosta (1920–2). Took part in the preparation of a monumental decoration of the town on the occasion of the first anniversary of the October Revolution. On his initiative a modern children's book-publishing firm was established. He invented a new method of designing children's books. Had numerous pupils and followers. In the 1920's and 1930's his works were often reprinted and discussed in foreign art periodicals, among others in *Gebrauchsgraphik.*

Lissitzky, El (Lazar)
1890–1941

Studied architecture in Darmstadt. In 1915 started his professional career as an architect, at the same time practising painting and graphic art. In 1919 was appointed professor at the School of Fine Arts in Vitebsk. In 1921 lectured at the Vkhutemas and participated in the work carried out at the Inkhuk. During his stay abroad Lissitzky and Ilya Ehrenburg set up the *Veshch-Objet-Gegenstand* (1922) periodical in Berlin. Lissitzky was in contact with the most outstanding representatives of the west European *avant-garde* and a member of the *De Stijl* group. When in Switzerland, he started the *avant-garde* journal *ABC* and made posters for the Pelikan firm. After his return to the Soviet Union (1925) he became head of the woodworking studio of the Vkhutemas. He was one of the first European designers to work out the method of aesthetico-functional analysis of industrial products. In 1927 started to design pavilions for home and international trade fairs. Lissitzky exerted a strong influence on contemporary graphic design, especially for mass publications. He experimented with the photomontage technique. Designed numerous experimental publications, books, catalogues, prospectuses and leaflets. For several years worked as art director for the editorial office of the *SSSR na Stroyke* (The USSR in Construction) periodical (1932–5).

Malevich, Kasimir
1878–1935

Graduated from the Academy of Fine Arts in Moscow. His works were exhibited, with others, at the exhibition of the 'Artists Association' (1907), the 'Donkey's Tail' (1912) and the 'Union of Youth' (1912). He designed costumes and settings for A. Kruchyonykh's futuristic opera *The Victory over the Sun* (1913), and covers and illustrations for volumes of futuristic poetry. His Suprematist works were for the first time displayed at the '0, 10' exhibition (1915). During the first months of World War I he designed colour pictures for soldiers made in the style of the lubok folk drawing. After the outbreak of the October Revolution he came to the fore of the *avant-garde* movement and collaborated with the People's Commissariat for Education in its endeavour to shape a new system of state patronage. When lecturing at the

School of Fine Arts in Vitebsk he organized the 'Unovis' art group (1920–1). In the same period he designed several posters and street decorations (e.g. the 'agit-tramway'). In 1922 organized the Institute for Artistic Culture in Petrograd (Inkhuk). In the period 1922–8, Malevich created his Suprematist compositions, the so-called 'architectons', and designed new forms of ceramic ware. In 1927 made a journey to Germany, passing through Warsaw. Published several theoretical studies. His *Suprematism* (Vitebsk 1920), written in Malevich's own hand with the use of dynamic graphic arrangements, was printed from linoleum blocks.

Mayakovsky, Vladimir
1893–1930

Graduated from the School of Fine Arts in Moscow. Belonged to the group of Futurist poets and was co-author of their manifesto: 'The Insult to Universal Taste' (1912). In 1913 he published, at his own expense, a volume of poetry called *Ja (I)* with illustrations by V. Chekrygin and L. Zhegin. Like Malevich, he also painted colour pictures for soldiers during the first months of World War I. Was one of the founders of the revolutionary posters workshop (Rosta Windows), and author of the majority of texts and drawings issued by it. During the period of the New Economic Policy (1923–5) he designed advertisements in partnership with Rodchenko. His short poems and drawings were printed in newspapers and formed part of propaganda posters. It was Mayakovsky who prepared the first and only issue of the *BOB* (The Jesters Fighting Division) satirical magazine to which he contributed the cover design and a few drawings. He also published a few booklets of the comic-strip type, such as: *A Story of the Deserter* (1921), *Down with Rot-gut* (1923), *The Rites* (1923), *Nobody Is Going to Help Us* (1923), and a political pamphlet published as *Mayakovsky's Gallery* (1923). He designed settings to his own plays: *The Mystery Bouffe* and *The Baths.*

Miller, Grigory
1900–58

Studied at the Painting Department of Vkhutemas. Together with Lissitzky, he designed the USSR's pavilion at the International Press Exhibition (Cologne 1928). Also designed protective garments for the Work Safety Institute and occupied himself with problems of modern industrial design. When designing books he made use of mobile models of his own construction. Made paintings and sculptures.

Moor (Orlov), Dmitry
1883–1946

Studied physics, mathematics and law at Moscow University. Actively participated in the 1905 Revolution. His early drawings and cartoons were printed in newspapers. Was member of the editorial board of *Budilnik*, the liberal paper. The period of his greatest creative activity occupied the years 1918–22. His works included propaganda posters, cartoons printed in *Pravda, Izvestya, Bezboshnik* and *Dayosh*. Designed 'agit-trains', providing them with appropriate texts. Lectured at the Graphic Art Department of the Vkhutemas.

Popova, Lubov
1889–1924

She studied painting in private studios. Travelled to Italy and France. Her works were displayed, among others, at the following exhibitions: 'Jack of Diamonds', 'Tramway V' (1915), '0, 10' (1915), 'Magazin' and '5×5=25' (1921). In the years 1921–4 she was a member of the Productivists Group. Together with A. Vesnin she designed street decorations on the occasion of the Third Congress of the International Socialist Movement and a model of the 'End of Capitalism' mass show. She headed the Colour Construction Studio of the Vkhutemas, actively participated in the work carried out at the Inkhuk and collaborated with the *Lef* group. For a certain time worked as stage designer in Meyerhold's theatre, preparing settings for *The Magnanimous Cuckold* (1922) and *The Earth in Turmoil* (1923). She collaborated with the textile industry, designing both fabrics and fashions, and occupied herself with poster-making and book-designing.

Prusakov, Nikolay
1900–52

Studied art at the First Free State Workshops and at the Vkhutemas. Was one of the members of the Association of Young Artists (Obmokhou) group. His works were exhibited at the First Polemical Exhibition of Revolutionary Art (Moscow 1924), organized by the first graduates from the Vkhutemas. Was industrial designer, poster-maker and author of exhibition arrangements. For a certain time worked together with Lissitzky. He was the organizer of the Second Film Posters Exhibition (1928).

Rodchenko, Alexander
1891–1956

Started to study art in Kazan; afterwards attended the Moscow School of Applied Arts (Stroganovka). His works were for the first time displayed at the 'Magazin' exhibition in 1916, and, a year later, he presented his three-dimensional compositions. Took part in designing interiors of 'Café pittoresque', the meeting-place of artists. After the outbreak of the October Revolution he joined a group of *avant-garde* artists and held the post of secretary of the Left-wing Federation of Moscow Artists Union. He played an important role in the Fine Arts Section of the People's Commissariat for Education. Together with Rozanova he set up its artistic handicrafts section. Was one of the founders of the Institute of Artistic Culture (Inkhuk). In 1920 was appointed professor of the Vkhutemas and, in 1922, became vice-dean of its Metalworking and Woodworking Department and head of the Basic Division. His works were displayed at numerous exhibitions including that organized on the occasion of the Third Congress of the Comintern (1920) and at the '5×5=25' exhibition at which he presented his mobile compositions. In 1923 entered into a wide-ranging artistic partnership with Mayakovsky. They even had their own trade-mark reading: 'Mayakovsky, Rodchenko – advertisement designers'. In 1922 Rodchenko started to work for publishing firms designing book covers, illustrations and posters. During the years 1923–30 he designed fourteen volumes of Mayakovsky's poems and gathered an extensive collection of photographs pertaining to the poet's life. In 1925 he designed a model workers' club interior displayed by the Soviet Union at the Art Déco exhibition in Paris. In 1924 he became interested in art photography and his works were printed in various periodicals. He also designed film and theatre settings; among others, he invented the first dynamic credits sequences to Dziga Vertov's documentary films. During the period 1933–41 Rodchenko, and his wife Varvara Stepanova, regularly contributed illustrative material to the *SSSR na Stroyke* (USSR in Construction) illustrated periodical produced for foreign readers. They provided all or at least a part of the illustrations to its thirteen issues including such special issues as: 'Belmostroy' (1935), 'Kazakstan' (1935), 'Parachuting' (1936), and that devoted entirely to Mayakovsky (1940). They also designed the following illustrated albums: *Ten Years of Uzbekhistan* (1934), *The First Cavalry Division* (1935–7), *The Red Army* (1938), *Soviet Aviation* (1939) and *The March of Youth* (1939).

Roskin, Vladimir
born 1896

Studied art at the Moscow School of Applied Arts (Stroganovka). Displayed his works at the Fifth Narkompros Exhibition (Moscow 1918). Together with Mayakovsky he made political posters for Rosta and designed street decorations on the occasion of revolutionary anniversaries. He assisted Lissitzky in designing the USSR's pavilion at the International Press Exhibition in Cologne (1928) and at Leipzig (1932). He was awarded the Grand Prix at the World Exhibition in Paris (1936) for his display design. He was linked with the *Lef* group.

Rozanova, Olga
1886–1918

She graduated from the Moscow School of Applied Arts (Stroganovka). Was closely linked with the group of Futurist poets and made illustrations to Khlebnikov's and Kruchyonykh's poems. She was the founder of the Union of Youth (Petrograd 1910) and exhibited her works at its collective exhibitions. Rozanova, Exter and Goncharova were three women artists who played an important role in the *avant-garde* movement. Rozanova's works were also exhibited at the 'Tramway V' and '0, 10' exhibitions. She was a member of the Department Council of IZO (Fine Arts Department) of the People's Commissariat for Education and, together with Rodchenko, organized its artistic handicrafts section.

Sedelnikov, Nikolay
born 1905

A typographer from Moscow. For a certain time worked jointly with S. Telingater. Carried out experiments aimed at applying photographic technique in typography. He is the author of several book covers designed with the use of typographic elements. In the 1930's he engaged in extensive correspor.dence with J. Tschichold.

Semyonova, Yelena
born 1898

Attended the First Independent State Studios and then studied sculpture and architecture at the Vkhutemas. Was associated with the *Lef* group and with the Inkhuk. As a result of differences in opinion she left *Lef* and abandoned her studies. Her view of the social role of an artist was close to that held by members of the

Productivists Group. She worked as stage designer at the 'Sinaya Bluza' (The Blue Overall) workers' theatre. Holding the post of chief designer of the Exhibition Bureau she designed several exhibition arrangements, such as 'Petrol' and 'New Living'. She ran a press column providing guidance in the field of interior design.

Senkin, Sergey
1894–1963

Attended the School of Fine Arts in Moscow. After the outbreak of the October Revolution continued his studies at the Vkhutemas from which he graduated in 1929. He was an active member of the students movement and then of the Party. In the years 1923–30 occupied himself with industrial design and collaborated with several publishing firms and periodicals. Together with G. Klutsis he made photomontages which illustrated publications devoted to 'Children and Lenin' and 'Lenin and Young People' (1924). In 1927–37 designed settings to mass shows commemorating revolutionary occasions. He made over a dozen propaganda posters and designed several exhibition arrangements. He assisted Lissitzky in designing photomontages which decorated the USSR's pavilion at the International Press Exhibition in Cologne (1928).

Stenberg, Georgy
1900–33
Stenberg, Vladimir
born 1899

Two sons of a Swedish-born artist. They studied art at the Moscow School of Applied Arts (Stroganovka) and then in the First Independent State Studios. They made posters, stage settings and exhibition arrangements, and took part in designing street decorations in Moscow on the occasion of the First of May and of the first anniversary of the October Revolution (1918). Their works were exhibited at exhibitions organized by the 'Association of Young Artists' (Obmokhu). Both brothers actively participated in the work carried out at the Inkhuk. In the years 1922–33 they designed numerous stage settings, among others for O'Neill's *The Hairy Ape* (1926, especially praised by Lunacharsky) and *The Negro* (1929), G. B. Shaw's *Saint Joan* (1924), and *Kukirol* (1925). For several years (starting with 1928) they decorated the Red Square in Moscow on successive anniversaries of the October Revolution. For their outstanding achievements as theatre designers the Stenberg brothers were awarded the Gold Medal at the Art Déco Exhibition in Paris (1925). During their stay in Paris in connexion with the appearances of the Kamerny Theatre they became acquainted with Larionov and Sonia Delaunay. In 1923 they started to make film posters, and in 1926 organized the First Film Posters Exhibition in the Kamerny Theatre, displaying their own works in an extremely original manner. Their posters received an award at the International Exhibition of Decorative Art in Monza-Milan (1927). In 1933 Georgy Stenberg was killed in a car accident.

Stepanova, Varvara (Varst)
1894–1958

Attended an art school in Kazan; continued her studies at the Moscow School of Applied Arts (Stroganovka). Her works were exhibited at the 'Fifth State Exhibition' (1918), 'The Tenth State Exhibition' (1919) and at the '5 × 5 = 25' exhibition (1921). She actively participated in the organization of art institutions and was president of the Union of Art Workers. In 1922 she started to work as designer (together with Popova) for the First Textiles Factory in Moscow. In 1924 was appointed professor in the Textiles Designing Department of the Vkhutemas. She was the author of several film and theatre settings, e.g., for *The Death of Tarelkin* (1922). She often worked together with her husband, A. Rodchenko.

Suetin, Nikolay
1897–1954

Studied art in Vitebsk under the guidance of K. Malevich. In 1923 became member of the State Institute of Artistic Culture (Ginkhuk) in Petrograd where, together with Malevich, he studied Suprematism and its applications in architecture. He then continued this research at the History of Art Institute in Leningrad (1927). For many years carried out experiments aimed at inventing new forms of ceramic ware for which he was awarded prizes in Milan (1925) and in Paris (1927). In 1932 he became interested in designing exhibition arrangements and created his own set of iterative elements known as 'suetons'. He designed the USSR's pavilion at the World Exhibition in Paris (1937) which was awarded the Grand Prix. Designed furniture, posters and book covers.

Telingater, Solomon
1903–69

He learned the art of drawing in Baku after which studied for a certain time at the Vkhutemas. In 1925 he started to work as a typographer. He learned the printing trade most thoroughly, working successively in all the printing departments. He was art director of several publishing firms. His works were exhibited abroad, among other places in Cologne (1928), Paris (1931), New York (1939), London (1955), Leipzig (1959, 1965, 1971), and Brno (1963). Designed books, posters, made photomontages; designed new type faces. Published several articles concerning the theory and methodology of typography. He received the Gutenberg Award in Leipzig in 1963.

Vesnin, Alexander
1883–1959

Studied technology in Petrograd. In 1918, together with his brother, Vasyl Vesnin, he decorated the Red Square in Moscow on the occasion of the First of May. His works were exhibited at the First Exhibition of Suprematist and Abstract Art (1919) and at the '5 × 5 = 25' exhibition (1921). In 1919 he became interested in stage design and made settings for the Children's and Kamerny theatres. His most outstanding stage designs include those for Chesterton's *The Man who was Thursday* and Racine's *Phèdre* (1923). In 1919 he was appointed professor of the Architecture Department of the Vkhutemas. From 1923 devoted himself mainly to architecture.

Bibliography

Books

A. Sidorov
Iskusstvo knigi. Moscow 1922

V. Polonsky
Russky revolutsyonny plakat. Moscow 1922

Russian Placards 1917–22.
Petersburg 1923

V. Arvatov
Iskusstvo i proizvodstvo. Moscow 1926

N. Punin
Noveyshye techenya v russkom iskusstve.
Leningrad 1927

V. Arvatov
Ob agitatsyonnom i proizvodstvennom iskusstve.
Moscow 1929

A. Gushchin
Izo-Iskusstvo v massovykh prazdnestvakh i
demonstratsyakh. Moscow 1930

A. Gushchin
Oformlenye massovych prazdnestv za 15 let
diktatury proletaryata. Moscow 1932

B. Livshits
Polutoraglazy Strelec. Leningrad 1933

B. S. Butnik-Siversky
Sovetsky plakat epochi grashdanskoy voyny
1918–21. Moscow 1960

Slovo o Pluku Majakovského. Liryka agitace poemy
dokumenty. Prague 1961

Y. Khalaminsky
D. Moor. Moscow 1961

N. Khardshyev
A. M. Rodchenko. Iskusstvo Knigi. Vypusk vtoroy
1956–7. Moscow 1961

C. Gray
The Great Experiment: Russian Art 1863–1922.
London 1962

N. Khardshyev
El Lissitzky-Konstruktor Knigi. Iskusstvo Knigi.
Vypusk trety. Moscow 1962

El Lissitzky
Kniga s tochki zrenya zritelnovo vospryatya-
visualnya kniga. Iskusstvo knigi. Vypusk trety.
Moscow 1962

V. A. Katanyan
Khudoshnik Vladimir Mayakovsky. Moscow 1963

Lubomir Linhart
Alexandr Rodčenko. Prague 1964

J. Křiž
Pavel Mikolajevič Filonov. Prague 1966

E. Semenova
Vkhutemas, Lef, Mayakovsky. Trudy po russkoy i
slavyanskoy filology. Vol. IX. Tartu 1966

W. Duwakin
Rosta Fenster. Dresden 1967

Zdeněk Mathauser
Die Kunst der Poesie Stufen, die zur Oktober-
Dichtung hinführten. Prague 1967

Sophie Lissitzky-Küppers
El Lissitzky Maler, Architekt, Typograf, Fotograf.
Dresden 1967. (English edition, London 1968)

Werner Schmidt
Russiche Graphik de XIX und XX Jahrhunderts.
Leipzig 1961

Troels Andersen
Moderne Russisk Kunst 1910–30. Copenhagen
1967

Vladimir Favorsky
Compiled and edited by Youri Molok (in English).
Moscow 1967

L. Volkov-Lannit
Alexander Rodchenko. Risuyet. Fotografiruet.
Sporit. Moscow 1968

Herta Wescher
Die Collage Geschichte eines Künstlerisch
ausdrückmittels. Cologne 1968

N. Khardshyev
Pamyati Natalyi Goncharovoy i Mikhaila
Laryonova. Iskusstvo Knigi. Vypusk 5. 1963–4.
Moscow 1968

Vladimir Markov
Russian Futurism: a history. Los Angeles 1968

Eberhard Steneberg
Russiche Kunst Berlin 1919–32. Berlin 1969

Sovetskaya Architektura
18 Sbornik Soyuza Architektorov SSSR.
Moscow 1969

Herbert Spencer
Pioneers of modern typography. London 1969

Agitatsyonno-Massovoye Iskusstvo Pervykh let
Oktyabrya. Materyaly i issledovanya. Moscow 1971

Magazines

Karel Teige
Sovětský Konstruktivismus. 'ReD', No.1, 1927,
Prague

Jan Tschichold
El Lissitzky, 'Imprimatur' III, 1930

Camilla Gray
El Lissitzky. Typographer. 'Typographica', 1960,
London

'Vytvarné Umeni', No.8/9, 1961, Prague

Szymon Bojko
Rodchenko and the origins of the avant-garde
movement in the USSR. 'Projekt', No.5, 1962,
Warsaw

Szymon Bojko
Aleksander Rodczenko o fotografii i Majakowskim.
'Fotografia', No.11, 1962, Warsaw.

Camilla Gray
Alexander Rodchenko: a Constructivist designer.
'Typographica', 1965, London

A. Abramova
Odna iz pervykh (about V. Stepanova).
'Dekorativnoye Iskusstvo SSSR', No.9, 1963,
Moscow

Y. Gerchuk
Telingater khudoshnik knigi. 'Dekorativnoye
Iskusstvo SSSR', No.3, 1964, Moscow

L. Abramova
Tradytsyi sovetskoy promgrafiki. 'Dekorativnoye
Iskusstvo SSSR', No.3, 1963, Moscow

A. Abramova
2 Stenberg 2. 'Dekorativnoye Iskusstvo SSSR',
No.9, 1965

A. Goncharov
Vkhutemas. 'Dekorativnoye Iskusstvo SSSR',
No.4, 1967

Szymon Bojko
Le dévancement d'une époque. 'Démocratie
Nouvelle', No.2, 1967, Paris

L. Shadova
Lyubov Popova. 'Technicheskaya Estetika',
No.11, 1967, Moscow

'Cimaise', No.85/86, Paris 1968

L. Marc
Propedevtichesky Kurs Vkhutemasa-Vkhuteina.
'Technicheskaya Estetika', No.2/1968, No.4/1968,
No.12/1968, Moscow

El Lissitzky
New Russian art – a lecture given in 1922.
'Studio International', October 1968, London

I. Uvarova
'Veshchy Tyanut k sebe v Noru.' 'Dekorativnoye
Iskusstvo SSSR', No.9, 1968, Moscow (about
Rodchenko)

Yury Gerchuk
Golos nemovo kino. 'Dekorativnoye Iskusstvo
SSSR', No.2, 1968, Moscow

L. Marc
Gustav Klutsis. 'Technicheskaya Estetika', No.1
1968, Moscow

COLLEGE LIBRARY
COLLEGE OF TECHNOLOGY
CARNARVON ROAD
SOUTHEND-ON-SEA, ESSEX

K. Volodin
'Veshch.' 'Dekorativnoye Iskusstvo SSSR',
No.5, 1968, Moscow

V. Strakhova
Sovremenno i ponyne (about A. Rodchenko).
'Tvorchestvo', No.2, 1969, Moscow

Szymon Bojko
Collages et photomontages oubliés de A.
Rotchenko. 'Opus International', No.10/11, 1969,
Paris

L. Shadova
Vkhutemas-Vkhutein.
'Dekorativnoye Iskusstvo SSSR',
No.11, 1970

L. Oginskaya
Gustav Klutsis khudoshnik leninskoy temy.
'Dekorativnoye Iskusstvo SSSR', No.4, 1970,
Moscow

Szymon Bojko
'Leniniana' w plastyce rewolucyjnej. 'Fotografia',
No.7, 1970, Warsaw

Alla Povelikhina
Old Russian Signboards. 'Projekt', No.4, 1970,
Warsaw (in English)

Yevgenyi Kovtun
Lithographed books by Russian Futurists.
'Projekt', No.6, 1970, Warsaw (in English)

L. Oginskaya
Khudoshnik – Agitator (about G. Klutsis).
'Dekorativnoye Isskustvo SSSR', No.5, 1971,
Moscow

S. Frederick Starr
Writings from the 1960s on the Modern
Movement in Russia. 'Journal of the Society of
Architectural Historians', No.2, volume XXX,
New York 1971

Catalogues

Exposition Internationale des Arts Décoratifs et
Industriels Modernes. Union des Républiques
Soviétistes Socialistes. Paris 1925

Vsesoyuznaya Poligraphicheskaya Vystavka.
Moscow 1927

Katalog des Sowjet-Pavillons auf der
internationalen Presse-Austellung. Cologne 1928

Solomon Benediktovich Telingater.
Khudoshnik knigi. Moscow 1963

Il Contributo russo alle avanguardie plastiche.
Galleria del Levante. Milano 1964

El Lissitzky
Kunsthalle, Basel 1966

Nowa sztuka czasów Rewolucji Październikowej.
Galeria Współczesna. Warsaw 1967

Międzynarodowy Plakat Rewolucyjny 1917–67.
'Zachęta'. Warsaw 1967

P. Filonov
Pervaya Personalnaya Vystavka. Akademgorodok.
Novosybirsk 1967

Agitatsyonno-Massovoye Iskusstvo Pervykh
Let Oktyabrskoy Revolyutsyi. Gosudarstvennaya
Tretyakovska Galereya, Moscow 1967

Russky estamp kontsa XIX – nachala XX veka.
Gosudarstvenny Russky Muzey. Leningrad 1967

Petrogradskye Okna Rosta. Gosudarstvenny
Russky Muzey. Leningrad 1968

Revolutionens Sprak. Moderna Museet.
Stockholm 1968

Die Fotomontage. Stadttheater Ingolstadt 1969

Malevich
Catalogue raisonné edited by Troels Andersen.
Stedelijk Museum. Amsterdam 1970

Katalog vystavki proizvedenyi Gustava Klutsisa.
Gosudarstvenny Khydoshestvenny Muzey
Latvijskoy SSR. Riga 1970

Russkye Narodnye Kartinki XVII – XVIII ve-kov.
Gosudarstvenny Muzey Izobrazitielnych Iskusstvim
A.S. Pushkina. Moscow 1970

Art in Revolution. Soviet Art and Design since
1917. Hayward Gallery. London 1971.

Russian Art of the Revolution. Brooklyn Museum
of Art, 1971

Art and Architecture. USSR. 1917–32. The Institute
for Architecture and Urban Studies. New York
1971

The Non-Objective World. 1924–39. Galerie Jean
Chauvelin. Paris 1971

Russian Avant-Garde 1908/1922.
Leonard Hutton Galleries, New York 1971